THE
STAINED GLASS
OF
NEW COLLEGE, OXFORD

THE BLESSED VIRGIN MARY
South-east Window of the Ante-Chapel

THE
STAINED GLASS
OF
NEW COLLEGE, OXFORD

BY

CHRISTOPHER WOODFORDE
LITT.D., D.LITT., F.S.A.

GEOFFREY CUMBERLEGE
OXFORD UNIVERSITY PRESS
LONDON NEW YORK TORONTO
1951

Oxford University Press, Amen House, London E.C. 4

GLASGOW NEW YORK TORONTO MELBOURNE WELLINGTON
BOMBAY CALCUTTA MADRAS CAPE TOWN

Geoffrey Cumberlege, Publisher to the University

PRINTED IN GREAT BRITAIN
AT THE UNIVERSITY PRESS, OXFORD
BY CHARLES BATEY, PRINTER TO THE UNIVERSITY

PREFACE

I HAVE received much help in the making of this book. First and foremost, Mr. R. L. Rickard, Sub-Librarian of the College, transcribed for me all the College archives that I have used and later collated the quotations in my book with the original documents. I have also benefited from his intimate knowledge of the history of the College. Mr. E. A. Gee has most generously allowed me to use his unpublished extracts from the archives of other Oxford colleges and has thereby enabled me to give a much clearer picture of the activities of the glass-painters than I could otherwise have done. Mr. J. H. Harvey has allowed me to draw upon his great knowledge of medieval craftsmen. Mr. Anthony Wagner, Richmond Herald, and the late E. A. Greening Lamborn have helped me concerning problems of heraldry. Messrs. Oliver R. Barrett and Roger W. Barrett, Dr. Frederick W. Hilles, and the Cambridge University Press have given permission for the quotation of the letter from Sir Joshua Reynolds to the Warden of New College on pages 44–5; and Miss Andrews and Messrs. Eyre & Spottiswoode for the extract from *The Torrington Diaries* on page 55. Messrs. James Powell and Sons (Whitefriars) Ltd., Miss Joan Howson, and Miss Mary de Putron, who have had so much of the glass through their hands in recent years, have readily placed their records at my disposal.

My debt to the published works of others is evident. It is pleasant and reassuring to build upon such well-laid foundations.

I have collected the illustrations for this work from many sources. These sources are acknowledged on the plates, but I should say here that the permission of the Controller of H.M. Stationery Office has been given for the reproduction of the photograph on plate XIII and of the arms of the College on the title-page. I am most grateful to all who allowed me to use their photographs; a book about stained glass is of little value unless it is adequately illustrated.

CHRISTOPHER WOODFORDE

NEW COLLEGE, OXFORD
July 1950

ABBREVIATIONS

Two abbreviations are commonly used in this book: AR. for Account Rolls and CD. for Chapel Drawer.

CONTENTS

LIST OF ILLUSTRATIONS

Coloured frontispiece

THE BLESSED VIRGIN MARY
South-east Window of the Ante-Chapel
From a painting by Charles Fredericks

Monochrome plates
(at end of book)

I

THE HISTORY OF THE GLASS

1. THE FOURTEENTH CENTURY TO THE SIXTEENTH CENTURY

THE foundation-stone of New College was laid on 5 March 1380, and the Society entered formally into possession of its buildings on 14 April 1386. The quadrangle must have been completed by that time and it may be assumed that the windows of the chapel and hall were wholly glazed, the windows of the library partially glazed, and the living-quarters protected against the weather.[1]

The building-accounts for this period have not survived, although there are some for the bell-tower and the cloister, the latter being consecrated on 19 October 1400. It is not possible, therefore, to give the exact date, order, and cost of the glazing. It is unlikely that elaborate details were set out before the foundation-stone was laid; only a plan would have been necessary for that. If about a year is allowed for the preparation of the foundations and another year for the buildings to rise to a height of ten feet, it would be at the beginning of the third year, at the latest, that the glazier would have known the number, shape, and size of the windows that he had to fill before the spring of 1386.

The chapel and hall form the north side of the quadrangle. The chapel has a choir of five bays and is lit by five large windows on each side. There is no east window because the wall is a party wall with the hall. The nave, which has been called the ante-chapel since the eighteenth century, is of two bays and is aisled. This plan, well suited to the requirements of a collegiate body, is thought to have originated here or to have had a fortuitous origin in the earlier chapel of Merton College.[2] It was repeated

[1] The hall, chamber, and oratory of the Warden's Lodgings were probably glazed from the beginning, for the glass was in need of repair by 1417 (AR. 59, Dom.). There are no records of the repair of glass in the other living-quarters for many years. The windows may have been filled with some material such as linen, paper, or parchment, stretched on framed wooden trellises and treated with oil and turpentine, wax, or tallow, to make it translucent. The accounts show that the windows of both vestries and of the butteries were glazed by the middle of the fifteenth century (AR. 77, Dom., and see below, p. 9). The subject of the filling of windows with materials other than glass is surveyed in J. A. Knowles's 'Leaded Lights and Ornamental Glazing', *Journ. British Society of Master Glass-painters*, vii. 134–8, 184–91; viii. 18–25.

[2] *Historical Monuments Commission: An Inventory of the Historical Monuments in the City of Oxford*, London, 1939, xxi.

B

later at All Souls and Magdalen, and, after the Reformation, at Oriel, Brasenose, and Wadham. The ante-chapel is lit by eight large windows.

Considerations of time and expense may have influenced the choice of subjects for the stained glass in the chapel: single figures beneath canopies could be produced more quickly and cheaply than elaborate scenes. The subject-matter will be discussed in detail below. At this point it is sufficient to say that in the choir the eighty main lights contained figures of saints and that in the ante-chapel the great west window contained a 'Tree of Jesse' with a 'Doom' above it; the two eastern windows, the Twelve Apostles in the upper main lights and four representations of the Crucified Christ with the Blessed Virgin Mary and St. John Evangelist in the lower lights; in the remaining windows, Old Testament prophets in the upper main lights and other Old Testament personages in the lower main lights.

The hall has three windows on the southern side and four windows on the northern side. The windows were probably filled with quarries, which may have been patterned. There may have been some heraldic glass also.

The library occupied the greater part of the upper story on the eastern side of the quadrangle. It was lit by nine windows upon either side. These windows, of which three remain more or less intact, are each divided by a mullion and transom into four lights. The upper lights were probably filled with patterned quarries as soon as the building was finished.[1] The lower lights have a double rebate inside. The inner rebate may have been filled at first with removable wooden frames over which was stretched some translucent material.[2] These frames could be removed during the summer months or when the room needed ventilation. An entry in the Account Rolls for 1402–3 reads:

'Et in x libris stauni [sic] emptis pro sowdura pro fenestris vitreis imponendis in libraria prec. librae iii d. ob., ii s. xi d. Et solut. pro factura xviii fenestrarum vitrearum et imposicione pro aliis xviii fenestris in ferramento, xviii s.'[3]

The outer rebate received wooden shutters, which could be opened out against the splays of the window or shut and bolted.

The College statutes twice emphasize that no one may throw stones, balls, or other missiles to the endangering of the glass in the windows. Rubric 25 mentions possible damage to glass windows, walls, and roofs. Rubric 63 deals with such pastimes

[1] See below, p. 96.   [2] See above, p. 1, fn. 1.   [3] AR. 25, Scac. & Lib.

in the hall and chapel as might injure the rood, statues, glass windows, pictures, and other rich works, especially the imagery set against the wall dividing the hall and the chapel.[1] It is interesting that in the earliest surviving draft of the statutes, which shows them as they were before 1388, glass windows are omitted from the list of things which may be damaged by riotous games; it is probably because the prevention of 'divers hurlings of stones, balls, and other things at the said wall on the said hall side' was the main purpose of the rubric 63.

The Account Rolls are not complete: those that survive do not tell of any work other than repairs to the glass from time to time for a century after the chapel and hall windows were first glazed. The glass in the great west window was not sufficiently supported when it was first put up and new iron-work had to be inserted in 1406–7:

'Et in factura xxiii librarum dim. ferri Collegii pro viii Counter barres pro magna fenestra Capelle ca' pro factura librae 1 d. qᵃ., ii s. iiii d. ob. qᵃ. Et in ii Cownter barrs emptis ad eandem fenestram ponderantibus vii libras dim. prec. librae cum factura ii d., xv d.'[2]

Similar work was done in Winchester College chapel in 1421–2:

'Et Johanni Dyrford Smyzth de Soka pro xl counterbarres ponderantibus iiiixx libras pro fenestris vitreis capelle, prec. libre i d. ob. q., xi s. viii d.'[3]

'Counter bars' must mean the light iron bars inserted horizontally at intervals in the lights. The glass panels were attached to them by flat strips of lead, which were soldered. These bars were usually called 'soudlets'.

Although there is no documentary proof, it is almost certain that the glazing of the chapel, hall, and library was undertaken by Thomas Glazier of Oxford. It is in connexion with the New College windows that his name first appears. His antecedents are unknown.[4] There were glass-painters resident in Oxford at

---

[1] *Liber Statutorum Collegii Beatae Mariae Wyntoniensis in Oxonia*, ed. 1797, 75, 157–8.

[2] AR. 33, Cap.

[3] J. D. Le Couteur, *Ancient Glass in Winchester*, Winchester, 1920, 117.

[4] In 1351–2 glass was painted for the windows of St. Stephen's chapel, Westminster. Glaziers were collected from all over the country for the work, and many of them stayed on to paint glass for the chapter house of St. George's, Windsor. Among them were Nicholas and Thomas Dadyngton, who were probably father and son. Deddington is between Oxford and Banbury. Attempts have been made to show that Thomas Dadyngton is identical with Thomas Glazier of Oxford (see H.J. Powell, 'The Picture-windows in New College Ante-Chapel', *Burlington Magazine*, viii. 329; Le Couteur, *Ancient Glass in Winchester*, 19–21; H. Read, *English Stained Glass*, London, 1926, 109;

least as early as the end of the twelfth century: the names
Geoffrey, Jordan, Thomas de Fretewel, and Walter occur between *c.* 1190 and *c.* 1270.[1] Thomas had a son of the same name
who flourished between 1258 and 1303. John Glazier was working between 1338 and 1374. The first mention of Thomas Glazier
in the New College records is in August 1386 when the Steward
of the Hall's Book records that he dined in hall. He had dinner
or supper in hall five times in 1387–8 and six times in 1388–9.
He continued to have meals in hall about four times a year for
the next ten years. From 1398 until 1422 he came only once or
twice a year, perhaps because of advancing years or ill health.
From 1388 onwards he is recorded as having meals with the
Fellows of the College. Occasionally his assistant was entertained
also. For instance, in December 1390 there is the entry:

'Thomas Glasyer et famulus suus venerunt eodem die ad prandium
cum sociis',

and in 1391:

'Thomas glasier et Rogerus socius suus vitriarius venerunt die
Vigilia Pasche ad prandium cum sociis.'

His last recorded work on the College windows was in 1416–
17, but he probably had charge of the glazing later than that.
The rolls for the succeeding years are not complete. He was
repairing the glass at Winchester College in 1421–2.[2] He was
dead by 1427–8: an entry for that year reads:

'Et solut. Relictae Thome Glasier' pro factura ii Casarum corporalium
cum nodulis aureis et fimbreis et tassellis de serico, xx d.'[3]

By about the end of the fourteenth century or the beginning
of the fifteenth century Thomas had completed the stained glass
for the chapel windows at Winchester College.[4] The roll of

&c.). The identification is very unlikely, as Thomas of Oxford did not die until after
1422. In 1322 William Aylmer, parson of Deddington, accused 'Thomas le Glasiere
with very many others' of house-breaking at Deddington and Caversham (*Cal. Patent
Rolls, 1321–4*, 155). As the above-mentioned Thomas Dadyngton was working at
St. Stephen's chapel as a glazier's mate breaking glass and grinding colours at the
rate of 4½d. a day it may be presumed that he was a youth and that the Thomas who
was concerned in the house-breaking was a relation, perhaps his grandfather.

[1] For most of the available information about these men see H. W. Garrod's
Ancient Painted Glass in Merton College, Oxford, London, 1931, 39–43.

[2] Le Couteur, *Ancient Glass in Winchester*, 117, quotes the following, '1421–2. In
solut. Thome Glasyer de Oxon. in partem solucionis liii s. iiij d. pro clarificacione et
reparacione fenestrarum tam in Capella quam in Aula, xvj s. vj d.'   [3] AR. 70, Cap.

[4] B. Rackham, 'The Glass of Winchester College Chapel', *Journ. British Society of
Master Glass-painters*, i, no. 4, 23–4, and *A Guide to the Collections of Stained Glass in the
Victoria and Albert Museum*, London, 1936, 50–1.

Wykeham's Household Expenses for 1393 includes the following:

'In expensis ii chariettorum de Esshere usque Oxoniam et de ibidem usque Clere et Wyntoniam cariantium vitrum pro fenestris Collegii domini Wyntonie per ix dies cum xii equis et vi hominibus chariettivis, xix s. iii d.'

The east window of the chapel at Winchester was filled with a 'Tree of Jesse' and the lateral windows with figures of saints beneath canopies. Between 1822 and 1828 Sir John Betton and David Evans of Shrewsbury took out the glass and replaced it by their own copy of it. At the bottom of the east window there are small kneeling figures of a carpenter, William Wynford the mason, Thomas Glazier, and Simon Membury, Clerk of the Works. Some of the original glass from the chapel survives in various places, but it does not include these figures.[1]

In February 1394 Thomas Glazier and Robert Keton, a Fellow of the College, were probably in London in attendance upon Wykeham:

'Et in expensis dicti Custodis equitantis ab Oxonia Londinium ad dominum Fundatorem de mandato suo directo per Robertum Keton' et Thomam Glasyer' a iiii° die februarii usque in xiiii diem eiusdem mensis videlicet per xi dies, xxii s. iii d. ob.'[2]

In the same year Thomas received the sum of 33s. 4d. 'for taking out and replacing' the glass in the chapel windows in Wykeham's residence at Highclere.[3] In 1395-6 he was doing

---

[1] See below, p. 102. The carpenter was probably Hugh Herland (fl. 1360–1405), who worked with William Wynford (fl. 1360–1404) at New College and Winchester, or one of the Hykenham family. (For Hugh Herland see J. H. Harvey, 'The King's Chief Carpenters', Journ. British Archaeological Association, third series, xi. 24–5.) William Wynford has been described as 'the architect of the Wells western towers, of Wykeham's colleges, of the Winchester nave, and perhaps of Wardour Castle' (see J. H. Harvey, Gothic England, London, 1948, 56). The Steward of the Hall's Book shows that both Hugh Herland and William Wynford dined at New College from time to time. They had sons at Winchester and New College: William Herland became a scholar of Winchester in 1393 and of New College in 1397: a Wynford, whose Christian name is unknown, became a Fellow of New College in 1396. Similarly, John Maydeston, who hung the New College bells, had a son Richard, who was admitted to Winchester in 1393 and a Fellow of New College in 1408. Simon Membury was Clerk of the Works of Winchester College. After holding many ecclesiastical preferments, he died c. 1423 and was buried in Salisbury cathedral, of which he was a residentiary canon. [2] AR. 14.

[3] William of Wykeham rebuilt the mansion at Highclere and regularly resided there. Wynford and Herland both worked there. Simon Membury was Rector of Burghclere, 1399–1402, and visited Highclere in 1396. See G. D. Dunlop, Pages from the History of Highclere, Hampshire, Oxford, 1940, 60: but he wrongly gives the date of the entry concerning Thomas Glazier as 1396 (57: compare Eccl. Commrs. Rolls 2/159403).

much work at Canterbury College. The manuscript which tells of his work is incomplete, but these entries remain:

'... ... pro vitriario   xl s.

... ... Thome glasyer lx s.'

'Item solutum Thome vitriario in plenam solucionem c s.'[1]

In 1397–8 settlement was made with him for work done in Adderbury church, Oxfordshire:

'In solut. Thome Glasier de Oxonia pro vitriacione iii fenestrarum in vestiario et i supra altare cum emendacione aliarum fenestrarum in domini cancello per manus Custodis, xiii s. iiii d.'[2]

In 1409–10 he was paid for work on the windows of St. Mary's church:

'Item pro vitriacione fenestrarum et pro vitro, vi s. viii d.

Solut. Thome Glasier pro arreragiis quantum ad opus vitriationis, xx d.'[3]

There is at present no other documentary record of his work, but some of the glass remaining in the clerestories of the nave of Winchester cathedral was probably painted by him.[4] In his will, made about a year before his death in 1404, William of Wykeham says:

'Item, Quia Deus decorem domus suae & locum habitationis suae diligit, ad honorem & laudem ipsius Dei, & Domini nostri Jesu Christi, & sanctae Mariae matris suae, Apostolorumque ejus Petri & Pauli, & Patronorum ecclesiae meae praedictae, nec non Sanctorum Birini, Swythuni, Eddae & Ethelwoldi, quorum corpora et reliquiae in dicta continentur ecclesia; volo & ordino quod Executores mei corpus sive medium ecclesiae supradictae inter alas australem & borealem, ab ostio occidentali chori ejusdem ecclesiae deorsum usque ad finem occidentalem ejusdem ecclesiae, in muris, fenestris & valto, honeste & honorifice, conformiter & decenter secundum exigentiam, formamque & modum novi operis alarum praedictarum nunc incepti, nec non & easdem alas per idem spatium in longitudine refici faciant, ac debite reparari usque ad summam Duarum Millium & Quingentarum Marcarum, si tantum expendi oporteat in opere supradicto, pro completione & consummatione ejusdem, juxta modum & formam superius limitat. [sic]

[1] W. A. Pantin, *Canterbury College, Oxford*, ii, Oxford Hist. Soc. Publications, N.S., vii. 143, 145.

[2] AR. Adderbury b. The advowson of Adderbury was granted to the College by William of Wykeham on 10 May 1381.   [3] Oriel College: Treasurer's Accounts, i. 22.

[4] C. Winston (*Memoirs Illustrative of the Art of Glass-Painting*, London, 1865, 65), whose opinion cannot be lightly set aside, says of this glass that it 'is of precisely the same character as the original glass now remaining in the north, south, and west windows of the ante-chapel of New College Chapel, Oxford'.

Item lego pro fenestris tam superioribus quam inferioribus partis australis ecclesiae praedictae per me reparatae, bene & honeste & decenter juxta ordinationem & dispositionem Executorum meorum vitriandis, Quingentas Marcas. Et volo quod fiant hujusmodi fenestrae vitreae incipiendo in fine occidentali ecclesiae praedictae in novo opere per me facto seriatim & in ordine usque ad completionem ac consummationem omnium fenestrarum dicti novi operis partis australis antedictae. Et si quid tunc de dicta summa remanserit non expenditum, volo quod circa fenestras alae borealis totaliter expendatur, incipiendo in fine occidentali ad primam fenestram novi operis per me facti, & sic continuando versus partem orientalem, prout de parte australi superius specialiter ordinavi.'[1]

The glass that remains shows clearly that Wykeham's instructions about the order in which the windows were to be glazed were not carried out. The windows of both clerestories of the nave were glazed before the windows of the aisle, the glass in the aisle windows being painted by another and a later hand. It has been suggested that the clerestory windows were glazed first because the scaffolding was still standing.[2]

It has been noticed that there is a resemblance between the figures which Thomas Glazier painted for the east window of Winchester College chapel and two figures of kings in the west window of Canterbury cathedral. The resemblance is not close enough to suggest that they came from the same hand or the same workshop: the Canterbury figures may have been designed at Westminster by Richard Savage, the King's Glazier.[3]

In the same year that the widow of Thomas Glazier was paid for the corporal cases, the name of John Glazier first appears in the New College accounts:

'Et solut. Johanni Glasier' pro reparacione i panelli in magna fenestra vocata Cabulwyndowe [Gable window] ex parte occidentali Capellae, iii s. iiii d.'[4]

The last reference to him occurs in 1456, almost exactly thirty years later, and concerns the same window:

'Et solut. Johanni Glasier pro reparacione Fenestrae de ly Jesse, ii d.'[5]

There are also records of John Glazier's activity at All Souls College, and they are of particular interest because so much of his handiwork survives there. In 1441-2 he received part

[1] R. Lowth, *The Life of William of Wykeham, Bishop of Winchester*, 2nd ed., London, 1759, appendix xvii, pp. xxxvi–viii.

[2] *Ancient Glass in Winchester*, 25.

[3] See B. Rackham, *The Ancient Glass of Canterbury Cathedral*, London, 1949, 20–1, 119.

[4] AR. 70, Dom.   [5] AR. 80, Cap.

mended the windows of the library and chapel at Merton College in 1494–5; in the accounts of that college he is called Henry Peynter.[1] In 1506–7 he received 8s. for repairing glass in the ante-chapel at All Souls College.[2]

The payment of 8d. for each shield was about the normal sum at that time. The same amount was paid to a glass-painter named Boston when he made fourteen 'scocheons' for Little Saxham Hall, Suffolk, in 1509.[3] In 1513 Richard Wright of Bury St. Edmunds contracted to paint much glass for St. John's College, Cambridge, and he agreed to receive 'for every Rose and purcolious within the said wyndowes viij d.'[4] The price of 7d. a foot for the other fifteen feet of glass which Yong supplied for the Chequer suggests that it also was painted. In 1485 'florysche glasse' was being supplied to Coldharbour, London, at 6d. a foot.[5]

The glazing accounts for the sixteenth century are a steady record of small payments for the repair of glass in the chapel, hall, and other parts of the College. Heraldic glass was painted for the hall in 1527, for the hall in 1534, and for the library in 1582:

1527. 'Item solut. vitri factori pro armis fundatoris et ēpi cant' positis in fenestra in aula, vi s. viij d.[6]

1534. 'Solut. vitriario pro sex pecys off Armys et pro theca, xvii s. iiii d.[7]

1582. 'Solut. for crests for the lybrary wyndowe, xii d.'[8]

An entry for 1546–7 is the first evidence that there was quarry-work in the hall windows, and it is shown again in 1572:

1546–7. 'Solut. vitriario pro 5 pedibus vitri prec. pedis ii d. ob., in toto xii d. ob. Solut. eidem pro 9 pedibus prec. pedis ii d., xviii d. Solut. eidem pro 12 quarellis, iiii d.[9]

1572. 'for mendinge of 8 quarrels, xi d.'[10]

In 1570 and 1572 the expression 'story work' is used in speaking of the chapel windows:

1570. 'Solut. vitriario, xii d. Solut. vitriario pro 30 pedibus storywork, xix s. iiii d.[11]

[1] Merton College Archives, No. 4012: Sub-warden's Account, 1494–5.
[2] Bursar's Account Roll, 1506–7.
[3] J. Gage, *The History and Antiquities of Suffolk, Thingoe Hundred*, London, 1838, 148–9.
[4] Willis and Clark, *Architectural History of the University of Cambridge*, &c., ii. 347.
[5] L. F. Salzman, 'Medieval Glazing Accounts', *Journ. British Society of Master Glass-painters*, iii. 29.
[6] AR. 171, Aul.   [7] AR. 179, Aul.
[8] AR. 256, Dom.   [9] AR. 202, Aul.   [10] AR. 241, Aul.   [11] AR. 238, Cap.

1572. 'for mendinge a pane of glasse in the Weste Wyndowe, ii s. vi d., for mendinge a pane of Storie worke, xx d.'[1]

It could be taken to mean figures, but here, as elsewhere, it is much more likely to mean the glass in the tracery lights.

The glaziers are seldom named. John Showlsmyth (al. Shoke-smyth) repaired windows on the southern side of the choir in 1541.[2] He had a tenement, belonging to Oriel College, in High Street.[3] 'Denyshe vitrearius' did some small repairs to the hall windows in 1542.[4] An Oxford glazier named John North was at work on the chapel windows in the following year.[5] In 1578 a glazier named Thwayt, al. Twaytes, is first mentioned: he had the constant care of the windows for the next twenty years.[6]

The chapel was subject to three iconoclastic attacks in the sixteenth century. The first two are laconically recorded in the Account Rolls:

1546–7. 'Solut. 4[or.] Famulis Magistri Plummer laborantibus circa frangendas et deponendas imagines in summo altari et reliquis partibus templi, x s. viii d.[7]

1558–9. 'Solut. 2[bus.] Laborantibus per quatuor dies destruentibus altaria capientibus quolibet die 9 denarios et ii d. ultra in toto vi s. iiii d. Solut. tollentibus picturas vi d. Solut. duobus destruentibus altaria laborantibus per 4 dies capientibus quolibet die ii d. in toto vi s. viii d. Solut. Doly destruenti imagines, vi d.'[8]

Even then it was not considered that a clean enough sweep had been made. Robert Horne, Bishop of Winchester, visited the College in 1567 and thereafter ordered:

'Item ut tabulata in Chorum Capellae dicti Collegii et navem eiusdem Capellae amoveantur et prosternantur, usque ad altitudinem sedilium eiusdem chori, utque omnes et singulae imagines ibidem olim stantes igni committantur.

Item ut amotis tegminibus partis Orientis chori eiusdem Capellae parietes ibidem obmurentur plane, dealbentur et sententiae sacrae scripturae ibidem scribantur.'[9]

The first attack on the ornaments of the chapel would seem to be directly connected with the Royal Articles and Injunctions of Edward VI (1547) and the second attack with the Royal

---

[1] AR. 241, Cap.   [2] AR. 192, Cap.
[3] C. L. Shadwell and H. E. Salter, *Oriel College Records*, Oxford Hist. Soc. Publications, lxxxv. 160.   [4] AR. 194, Aul.
[5] AR. 197, Cap.; W. H. Turner, *Selection from the Records of the City of Oxford, 1509–1583*, Oxford, 1880, 173.
[6] AR. 248, Cap.   [7] AR. 205, Cap.   [8] AR. 226, Cap.
[9] New College Injunction Book, Injunctions 54–5.

Injunctions of Elizabeth (1559). If there had been any general destruction of the glass at these times or after Bishop Horne's visitation, the College records would certainly reflect it in subsequent heavy payments for glazing. There is no indication of extensive reglazing. It must be remembered that the removal of images and organs was one thing and the destruction of large areas of glass was another. Henry VIII's Injunctions of 1536 and 1538 and the Articles of Edward VI do not order the destruction of stained glass. It first appears in the Edwardian Injunctions of 1547. Although these Injunctions were imperfectly and spasmodically obeyed, there was enough destruction of glass to cause dismay and to warn the authorities that the buildings and services would suffer too much from unglazed windows. So Article 23 of the 1559 Injunctions, while repeating Article 28 of the 1547 Injunctions, adds the caution that the walls and glass must be preserved or repaired. This was re-emphasized in a subsequent Royal Proclamation.[1]

Nevertheless, it may have been in the second half of the century that the four crucifixes in the lower parts of the eastern windows of the ante-chapel were smashed, and perhaps their destruction is shown by this entry for 1564:

'Solut. vitriario pro novo vitro et pro reparatione scripturarum et imaginum, xxix s.'[2]

2. THE SEVENTEENTH CENTURY

The record of patching and mending continues throughout the seventeenth century. The most important entries in the first half of the century are those for 1628–9 and 1634–5:

'So. to the Slatter and other workeman for sweeping down the windowes of the Church and pointing them ut per billam, 13 s. 5 d. So. to a Dutch Pencill man for making newe 18 faces in the Church windowes some which were wanting others were broken or defaced at 6 s. 8 d. the face, £5. 17 s. o d. So. eidem for iii faces of pencill glasse that were putt into the garments of the pictures, 3 s. So. to 3 Slatters for pointing the Church windowes 5 dayes and a halfe 16 s. 8 d. So. to the Glasier for newe leading and binding and mending the Church windowes ut per billam, £13. o. o.'[3]

[1] For the above-mentioned Articles and Injunctions, see W. H. Frere and W. McC. Kennedy, *Visitation Articles and Injunctions of the Period of the Reformation*, 3 vols., Alcuin Club Collections, xiv–xvi. The Proclamation is quoted in C. J. Cox and C. B. Ford, *The Parish Churches of England*, London, 1935, 18.

[2] AR. 231, Cap.

[3] AR. 6–7 Charles I, Cap.

'So. to Mr. Vanlinge for 25 peeces of glasse for the librarie windowes and one face ut 4 s. a peece, £5. 0. 0.'[1]

An interesting parallel to these entries is in a letter from a Mr. Thomas Langton, who was interesting himself in the provision of new stained-glass windows for St. Paul's cathedral, to the Warden of Wadham College in 1621. In it he proposes that the young glass-painter Bernard van Linge shall be employed to paint the glass for the east window of Wadham College chapel. He says, 'I have sene his draufts and is an excellent Pensill man and of sober and good carriage not given to Drinke'. He gives a rough estimate of the cost, based on the supposition that 300 square feet of glass will be needed to fill the window, and goes on, 'so the workeman's work for so much & his pensill collers will amonte unto at 3ˢ 4ᵈ the foote is £50. 0. 0.'[2]

The use of the word 'face' in the first New College entry is curious. The scribe probably wrote 'faces' instead of 'pieces' in the sentence 'So. eidem for iii faces of pencill glasse that were putt into the garments of the pictures'. It can then be seen that the Dutchman charged 6s. 8d. for a new face (head) and 1s. for each piece of painted glass for the garments. In the second entry the scribe appears to have forgotten to put down the price of the head.

It is unfortunate that the College has not retained any of van Linge's glass. Bernard and Abraham van Linge, who were members of a family of glass-painters at Emden, were, with Baptist Sutton, the best known of the glass-painters who were encouraged by Archbishops Abbot and Laud to settle in England.[3] The van Linges left England upon the outbreak of the Civil War, but not before they had produced much stained glass, most of which is in Oxford. Bernard van Linge's window in Wadham College chapel is signed and dated 1622. He was responsible for the glass in the side windows of Lincoln College chapel and the figure of Bishop King in the cathedral.[4] Abraham van Linge, whose work is markedly different from and somewhat inferior to Bernard's, produced much glass for the cathedral in 1630; of this the picture of Jonah at Nineveh alone remains. He painted some windows

[1] AR. 10–11 Charles I, Lib.

[2] The letter and the contract between Wadham College and van Linge are printed in T. G. Jackson's *Wadham College, Oxford*, Oxford, 1893, 163–6.

[3] Bernard van Linge had been working in Paris for four years before coming to England.

[4] It is remarked in *Historical Monuments Commission: an Inventory of the Historical Monuments in the City of Oxford*, p. xxix, that in several cases the figures in the chapel of Lincoln College are duplicated in the windows of Lincoln's Inn chapel and that the background of the figure of Bishop King in the cathedral is also duplicated there: see also F. S. Eden, *Ancient Stained and Painted Glass in London*, London, 1939, 27–8.

for the chapel of Queen's College in 1635; this glass was reset in the new chapel by Joshua Price in 1715–17.[1] His windows in the chapel of University College are signed and dated 1641. It was probably he who supplied the glass for New College.

Occasionally the glazing accounts reflect the times in which they were written: in 1624–5 there is the entry, 'So. to the glasier for mending windowes in the Parliament tyme ut per billam, £1. 2 s.' and in 1646–7, 'So. to Barnard Rawlyns for re-payring the Vale windowes broken by the Ammunition, 6 s. 8 d.'[2]

Sometimes the accounts are detailed enough to give a clear indication of contemporary glazing costs:

1602 'So. to the Glasier for 4 quarrells of glasse, 4 d.'[3]

1615 'So. for the glasiar for ix foote of glasse new leaded at vi d. the foote, iiii s. vi d.'[4]

1617 'So. for 96 peeces of coloured glasse at 2 d. the peece, 16 s.'[5]

1632–3 'So. to the Plummer for newe leading 18 foote of glasse, 4 s. 6 d. So. for sodering and banding 9 foote more, 1 s. 1 d. ob. So. for 20 quarrells, 1 s. 8 d. So. for 30 quarrells, 2 s. 6 d. So. for sodering and banding 14 foote, 1 s. 9 d.'[6]

1636–7 Chapel. 'So. for newe leading 10 foote of pencill worke at 6 d. the foote, 5 s. So. for 3 peeces of colloured glasse, 9 d. So. for 70 quarrells in the Grammar schoole, 5 s. 10 d. So. for newe leading 12 foote of plaine worke at 3 d. the foote, 3 s. So. for repairing 6 foote at 1 d ½. the foote, 9 d. So. for 4 foote and halfe of newe glasse, 2 s. 6 d. So. for 28 pound of Soder and ½ at 10 d. the pound, £1. 3 s. 4 d.

Hall. '2° term. So. for newe leading 18 foote at 3 d. the foote, 4 s. 6 d. So. for 24 quarrells, 2 s. So. for repayring 8 foote of glasse, 1 s. So. for newe leading of 8 foote more of glasse, 2 s. So. for 8 quarrells more, 8 d. So. for repayring 4 foote of glasse, 6 d.

'3° term. So. to Fletcher for 18 quarrells of glasse in the Hall, 1 s. 6 d. So. for repayring 8 foote, 1 s. So. for newe leading 3 foote, 9 d.

'4° term. So. for 23 quarrells and repairing 24 foote, 4 s. 11 d. So. for newe leading 11 foote and repairing 6 foote, 3 s. 6 d. So. for 12 more quarrells, 1 s.'[7]

An entry for 1622–3 reads:

'So. for 10 foote of wire lettise for the windowe at the Hall-staires at 7 d. the foote. and 2 d. in tenter hooks, 6 s.'[8]

---

[1] See below, p. 19.

[2] AR. 23 James I–1 Charles I, Dom.; AR. 22–3 Charles I, Dom. 'The Vale' was the name given to a set of Fellow's rooms, which was probably on staircase 4 in the Old Quadrangle.   [3] AR. 44 Elizabeth–1 James I, Aul.   [4] AR. 12–13 James I, Aul.

[5] AR. 14–15 James I, Cap.   [6] AR. 8–9 Charles I, Aul.

[7] AR. 12–13 Charles I, Cap. & Aul. At this time the school for the choristers was situated between the chapel and the cloister. It was demolished in 1779.

[8] AR. 20–1 James I, Aul.

The use of wire guards to protect glass goes back at least as far as 1445. In that year 6s. 10d. was paid 'for makyng of iij grete latises set in the kyngges chappelle ther for conservacion of iij glason wyndowys, of wech a pece of latyzys holdyth vj foote in length and j foote and di' in brede, le foote iij d.' in the royal palace of Clarendon, Wilts.[1]

The entries for the second half of the century are not illuminating. This cryptic entry for work done in the chapel is tantalizing in its brevity:

1657 2° term 'Sol. to the Glazier for the exchange of Eight Tunn. 12^c 2^{qu} 16^{lb} at 3^s. 6^d. per hundred ut per billam   ...   £30–2–0
'Sol. to the Glazier for 46^{lb} of Soder ut per billam   ...   .   £1–18–11'[2]

There were also a number of payments for the glazing of other parts of the College. A large sum of money paid in 1675 suggests the completion of an extensive scheme for the glazing of windows which had hitherto been unglazed or partially glazed:

1675 4° term 'Sol. to Bernard Rawlins for the residue of lead Glass to the Library and the other chambers   ...   .   £32–16–1'[3]

At this point it is worth looking back and noting the periodic cleaning of the windows of the chapel and hall. The first record of such work occurs in 1527:

'Et solut. clericis pro purefactione fenestrarum, ix d.'[4]

In 1533–4 the windows of the hall were thoroughly cleaned:

'Solut. vitriario pro purgatione xxi pedum vitri fenestre aulae prec. pedis 1 d. ob., in toto ii s. vii d. ob. Solut. vitriario purganti cxvii pedes vitri prec. pedis 1 d. ob. in toto xiiii s. vii d. ob. Solut. vitriario purganti clxxxiiii pedes vitri prec. pedis ut supra, in toto xxxiii s.'[5]

In 1582 the chapel windows were cleaned:

'So. for besomes & sweeping the church wyndowes 2° et 3° ter. x d.'[6]

In 1610 three entries suggest that the leading of the glass in the chapel was in a fragile condition and that the cleaners were energetic:

'So. for ii men three days worke sweeping the Church windowes and for broomes, vi s.
So. for daming up the window ii men one daye, ii s.
So. for mendinge the glasse windowes, xvii s. vi d.'[7]

---

[1] Salzman, 'Medieval Glazing Accounts', *Journ. British Society of Master Glass-painters*, iii. 28.
[2] Bursar's Long Book, 1657.   [3] Ibid. 1675, Dom.   [4] AR. 171, Cap.
[5] AR. 179, Aul.   [6] AR. 254, Cap.   [7] AR. 7–8 James I, Cap.

As has already been noticed, in 1630–1 the slater and other workmen were paid 'for sweeping down the windowes of the Church and pointing them', and in the following year the glazier was paid 12s. 'for the remainder of a bill for worke done in making cleane the church windowes'.[1]

Apart from Abraham van Linge, four glaziers are mentioned by name during this century: James Fletcher, 1627–43: Bernard Rawlins, 1646–84: James Henning (al. Heming, Hemans), 1688–92: Charles Cole (al. Coles), 1696–1707. As is so often the case, it is impossible to say when 'glazier' ceased to mean 'glass-painter' and is used in the modern sense of the word. Fletcher supplied 'painted glass' for the hall in 1641, but there is no indication that he himself painted it.[2] The College evidently did not think him capable of producing new heads for the figures in the chapel, for van Linge was brought in for that.

3. THE EIGHTEENTH CENTURY TO THE TWENTIETH CENTURY

The beginning of the eighteenth century saw the chapel windows much as they were when they were first glazed. There had been patching and mending at various times, and some of the later glass, such as van Linge's heads and the 'coloured glass' introduced in the seventeenth century, may have looked incongruous enough. The gaps, especially in the figure-work, were probably many and serious both in the choir and ante-chapel. Yet, when full allowance has been made for all this, there was considerably more fourteenth-century glass than there is now and it was in its right place. By the end of the century the windows had been smitten so hard by three waves of enthusiastic generosity that the College is fortunate to have retained any medieval glass at all. The chapel now contains some of the most important examples of eighteenth-century glass-painting in the country, but the windows would be more acceptable if their erection had not meant the removal and loss of so much original glass.

The windows on the south side of the choir were tackled first. Unfortunately, there are only a few documents which throw light on the work. The first is as follows:

'Article of Agreement with William Price. Dec. 4. 1736.

It is hereby articled & agreed this fourth day of December 1736 by & between Mr William Price of Kirby Street, Hatton Garden, Glass Painter his Executors or Assigns on the one part & John Coxed, Warden

---

[1] AR. 6–7, 7–8 Charles I, Cap.   [2] AR. 17–18 Charles I.

of S[t.] Mary College of Winchester in Oxford commonly calld. New College in Oxford on behalf of himself & the Scholars of the said College & their Successors in manner & form following.

First it is articled & agreed between the said Parties & the said Mr William Price doth article and agree to & with the said John Coxed. That he the said Mr Price his executors or assigns shall & will New make execute & put up & fix the Windows lately taken down by him in the said College Chapel in such manner & with such material (viz.) with Glass & Lead, Putty etc of equal goodness, substance & thickness & with like Workmanship of painting, staining & colouring with the Window already made & fixed up by the said Mr William Price before Michaelmas Day next after the date of these presents. Also that the said Mr William Price shall & will at his own Costs & charge pay the expence of carrying the Old Glass Lead etc from Oxford to London to his own House. And that the said Warden & Scholars shall & will pay the like Expences of bringing the New Window when made from London to Oxford the same being first packed up at the costs & charges of Mr William Price.

Also it is further articled & agreed that the said Mr William Price shall not charge or reckon any further sum or sums of money for journeys or time spent by himself or others in taking down packing or otherwise preparing the old Glass Lead etc for Carriage to London. Or in packing sending down & fixing in workmanlike manner the New Glass Lead etc. over & above the consideration money for the whole work hereinafter mentioned.

And it is articled & agreed by & between the said Parties & the said John Coxed doth article & agree that the said Warden & Scholars for the time being shall & will pay or cause to be paid to the said Mr William Price the full sum of Sixty Three pounds as soon as the said Window is compleatly finished put up & fixed in manner aforesaid. And the said Mr William Price doth article & agree to accept the said Sixty Three pounds in full payment & satisfaction for the whole Workmanship Materials & charges incidental to the same.

Lastly it is articled & agreed between the said Parties & the said John Coxed doth article & agree on the part & behalf of himself & the Scholars of the said College & their Successors to give the said Mr Price the Sum of Twenty one pounds over & above the said Sum of Sixty three pounds if the said Window shall be compleatly finished put up & fixed in the Chapel of the College aforesaid before Michaelmas day next after the Date of these presents. And it is articled & agreed between the said Parties & the said Mr William Price doth article & agree to quit all manner of claim to the last mentioned Twenty one pound & the said Mr William Price doth hereby acquit discharge & release the said John Coxed the Warden & Scholars aforesaid & their Successors from payment of the said Twenty one pound or any part thereof if the said Window shall not be compleatly finished put up & fixd in the Chapel

c

aforesaid before Michaelmas day viz the Twenty Ninth day of September next after the date of these Presents.

Dec. 4ᵗʰ· 1736.   Willᵐ Price
   Witnesses   John Coxed
     Joseph Stevens
     John Hurst

N.B. All Scaffolding & Wiring is to be at the expence of the College. J.C.'

The following is added to the above agreement:

'Jan 7. 1739.

I do engage & agree to put up the fifth Window of the Chappel before or after Michaelmas day next on the terms & in the manner agreed on Dec. 4ᵗʰ· 1736.

                   Willᵐ Price'.[1]

Price was paid £84 for each of the five windows, receiving the first payment on 27 June 1735, and the last on 16 September 1740.[2]

Another document is a plan of the windows on the south side of the choir, with names of saints written in many of the lights. The plan was made by John Purnell, Warden, 1740–74, who added this note:

'Saints & Bps. painted in our Chappel—the Names by some great mistake left out when the Windows were new done.

N.B. Mr. Price told me this year (1746) in London that he could easily put them all in.'

The saints are as follows:

I. Upper tier. 1. *Thomas*.[3] 2. *Stephanu'*. 3. Blank. 4. *Xpofonus* (sic).[4] Lower tier. 1, 2, 3, 4. All blank.

II. Upper tier. 1. *Georgius*. 2. *Dionisius*.[5] 3. *Vincēcius*. 4. -*cencius*.[6] Lower tier. 1. *Titus*.[7] 2. *Abundius*.[8] 3. *Ignatius*.[9] 4. *Narcissus*.

---

[1] CD. 51.   [2] Building Chest Account.

[3] Price's figure is of a bishop. He was probably St. Thomas Becket.

[4] St. Christopher.

[5] Probably St. Denis of Paris. He shared an altar with St. George in Salisbury cathedral. Hyde abbey, in Winchester, possessed relics of the two saints, who are named together: see below, pp. 69–70.

[6] St. Laurence, as Price's figure shows and as might be expected.

[7] St. Paul's disciple. He was supposed to have been the first Bishop of Crete. There is a figure of Timothy in Winchester College chapel.

[8] See below, pp. 69–70. It is not possible to say which saint of this name was represented here.

[9] Part of his name is now in the west window of the north aisle of the ante-chapel: see below, p. 72.

III. Upper tier. 1. Blank. 2. *Situ.*[1] 3. *Sebastian.* 4. *Columnus.*[2] Lower tier. 1. *Christina.* 2. *Petronillos.* 3. *Katherina.* 4. *Margareta.* IV. Upper tier. 1. *Dannaas.*[3] 2. *Johēs M^{n}.* 3. *Paulus M^{n}.*[4] 4. *Aban' M^{n}.*[5] Lower tier. 1. *Agatha.* 2. *Lucia.* 3. *Cecilia.* 4. *Agnes.*[6] V. Upper tier. 1. *A . . .*[7] 2. *Oswald M^{n}.*[8] 3. *Edmundus M^{n}.* 4. *Reuchu'.*[9] Lower tier. 1. *Atheldrida.*[10] 2. *Helena.* 3. *Petronilla.*[11] 4. Blank.

William Price was the son of Joshua and nephew of William Price. From his father and uncle he learnt and inherited his business. They had painted glass for Oxford colleges. Joshua, who died in 1717, repaired and reset the earlier glass in the chapel of Queen's College in 1715–17 and painted its east window. He also repaired van Linge's glass in the cathedral. William Price the elder, who died in 1722, painted the east window of the cathedral in 1696 and of Merton College chapel in 1711–12. Fragments of the cathedral window are preserved in the clerestory of the transept. The Merton window has been removed but is extant.[12] The chief works done by William Price the younger before his New College windows were the rose window (1722) and the west window (1735) of Westminster abbey. He died at his home in Great Kirby Street, Hatton Garden, on 16 July 1765.

At the bottom of the fourth light of the lower tier of the westernmost window Price wrote *W. Price has Fenestras reparavit. A° D^{ni} 1740*. It is impossible to say how much of the original glass

[1] St. Sitha.   [2] Probably St. Columbanus: see below, p. 70.

[3] Perhaps St. Dunstan; but the other figures in the upper tier of this window are of martyrs, and Price's figure is of a pope.

[4] SS. John and Paul are said to have been martyred at Rome in 362: there is a basilica erected in their names on the Coelian Hill: see below, p. 70.   [5] St. Alban.

[6] In the plan the names in lights 2, 3, 4 are crossed out and the names Margaret, Agnes, and Cecilia are substituted.

[7] Possibly St. Amphibalus. There is a tradition that in pre-Conquest times he shared the dedication of Winchester cathedral. Bodies, supposed to be those of the saint and his companions, were discovered in 1178 (Matthew Paris, *Chronica Majora*, ii, ed. H. R. Luard, Rolls Series, 1874, 306–8). Richard Lee, Portcullis and deputy of Robert Cooke, Clarencieux, made a visitation of the county of Oxford in 1574. He saw in a window of St. Mary's church, Oxford, 'iij saints together' with their names 'Santa Albanus, prothomartir anglie', 'St. Phibalus', 'St. Oswyn, Rex et Mart.' over shields bearing their supposed arms. (*The Visitations of the County of Oxford*, &c., ed. W. H. Turner, Harleian Society Publications, v. 79.)

[8] King Oswald, who fell in the battle of Maserfield in 642.

[9] Possibly St. Richard, Bishop of Chichester, 1197–1253, but Price depicts a pope.

[10] In the plan the name is crossed out.

[11] In the plan the name is crossed out and St. Etheldreda's is substituted.

[12] *Historical Monuments Commission: an Inventory of the Historical Monuments in the City of Oxford*, xxix; H. M. Hake, 'Some Contemporary Records relating to Francis Place, Engraver and Draughtsman, with a Catalogue of his Engraved Work', *Walpole Society Publications*, x. 65.

remained in London besides the names, which were never put back. As will be seen, Price incorporated in his windows some old glass, including canopies; but a great deal more must have gone to London than ever came back.[1]

It was the intention of the College at this time to deal next with the windows on the north side of the choir. There is some evidence for this in the following:

'Extract of Mr. H. Coker's Will as far as concerns New Coll: Will Dated the 1st Sept. 1749.

Item I do give & bequeath to the Warden & Fellows of New College the sum of one Hundred Pounds upon Condition that they will repair & beautifie two Windows of the North side of the inner Chappel within four Years after my Death. Those nearest the Organ, fifty pounds to be paid upon finishing the first Window, Fifty pounds more on finishing the second.'[2]

There was, however, a change of plan, and the College turned its attention to the great west window. It was decided that William Peckitt of York should be asked to fill it with glass of his painting.[3] The correspondence relating to the work is lost, but the following undated documents must refer to it:

'Mr Peckett's Estimate of his Expenses.

569½ sq^r Feet of Glass is the measure of the whole window in the clear. The last sum agreed upon was £400, and the old window.

Out of the above sum £30 is allowed for 60 sq^r feet of stone work that was intended to have been cut away.

Allso £5 is allow^d for Interest of the receiv^d one Hundred pounds.

My expences exterordnary in journeys, loss of time, Drawings, cases, carriage of the Glass, etc costs me allso out of the above £110.

So I receive only about 10^s p^r foot square for the Lights of Glass.'[4]

'Mr Peckett's Estimate of his Expenses	£
All the Drawings to be made will cost me at least	40
The Cases, package, Carriage, porterage, etc of the compleated Glass from York to Oxford will cost	10
My Time from home, Traveling expences, when I return to, and go from Oxford when the window is put up; and allso in part at present will cost me at least as I can make it appear...	50
I alow for the Old Glass	30
Its carriage to York will cost me	8'[5]

---

[1] The tradition of the Flemish origin of some of the glass is discussed below, p. 66.

[2] Upper Muniment Room. Benefaction Drawer. The College did not receive the legacy until 1774.

[3] The life and work of William Peckitt, 1731–95, have been carefully surveyed in J. A. Knowles's 'William Peckitt, Glass-painter', *Walpole Society Publications*, xvii. 45–59.   [4] CD. 76.   [5] CD. 77.

The 'old glass' which Peckitt took in part payment for his new window was the 'Tree of Jesse'. It is not known how complete that window was when he took it out, but some of the panels thereafter passed to York minster where they may still be seen in the third window from the west in the south aisle of the choir.[1]

The new window was largely paid for from a bequest by John Eyre, who became a Fellow of New College in 1741. In his will, which was proved on 8 December 1762, he said:

'I hereby give to the Warden Fellows and Schollars of New College Oxford in Oxford the sum of three hundred Pounds to finish the West Window facing the Organ in the Ante-Chapel of the said New College in the same manner as the New Windows in the Inner Chapel are finished and if the said Sum of three hundred Pounds be not disposed of in the manner herementioned within five years after my Death I then give and bequeath the Said Sum of three hundred Pounds to my Executor hereinafter appointed.'[2]

The inscription in the window shows that Peckitt completed it in 1765.

It was decided that Peckitt should next fill the three western-most windows of the choir, but, as the following correspondence shows, the College was dissatisfied with his figure-work and was determined to find a competent artist to make drawings or cartoons for him to copy.

'Mr Peckett's Proposals

Proposals to execute or paint in Glass the Windows on the North side of the inner Chapel of New College, in the Best Manner in Figures, their pedistals & other Ornaments; all properly finished with strong Glass, well leaded, soderd & cemented, at the rate of Twenty five pounds pr Figure. And cleane, repair, & new lead the old Croket Lights in each window, for five pounds.

If two windows are done and put up at one time, the Gentlemen must please to allow me forty pounds and the two old windows to defray my exterordnary expences for Drawings, journey, loss of time, cases, carriage, Risque, etc. I delivering them safe at the College, and wait a reasonable time to see them placed aright. The College to be at the expence of scaffolding, and putting the Glass up.

One Hundred pounds part of the above as usualy must be remitted me Interest free within two months after my ingagement, for security

[1] See Chap. IV.

[2] Upper Muniment Room. Benefaction Drawer. His brother Edward Eyre was his sole executor. The 'New Windows in the Inner Chapel' are, of course, Price's.

I give my own Bond. And to compleat the two windows God give leave within two years from the date of ingagement.

Expences of each new Window

	£
Eight large Figures	200–0–0
Crocket Lights	5–0–0
Old Windows	25–0–0
Journey, Drawings etc.	20–0–0
	250–0–0'[1]

With Peckitt's 'Proposals' is another document which, like Mr. Coker's will, shows that the reglazing of these windows had been under consideration for some time:

'A note of Mr. Peckitt's proposals.
There is not so much difference between Mr. Peckitt's present proposals & those delivered to Warden Hayward some years ago, as I imagined.

Besides the Old Glass, Proposals to Warden Hd.	225–0–0
Present proposals	231–0–0
Difference	6–0–0'[2]

In 1766 Peckitt had completed the great west window of Exeter cathedral.[3] The College sought the advice of the Dean about designs for their own windows.

The Dean of Exeter to Henry Bathurst[4]

Exeter Dec^r· 28th· 1771.

S^r

I am favoured with your letter & shall think myself very happy, if my opinion, or advice can contribute in any respect to the improvement of the design, which your College is now undertaking & which, if well executed, will be a great embellishment to your chappel. Every one who has seen the two windows, wch Pecket executed for your College & this Cathedral, has lamented the want of a skilfull draughtsman in the former of those works, & nothing has done Mr Peckitt so much credit, as the Cartoons from which he painted our figures. They were not originally his own property or procuring, but were part of a purchase he made of the Ex^{rs} of the late famous Artist Mr. Price. He made no other alterations in them, than adapting the proper emblems to the characters required. He had others of the same kind, which might answer your purpose very well, provided the figures you want for your windows are to be Apostles or Saints, but even in that case I would

---

[1] CD. 74.
[2] CD. 75.
[3] Reproductions of Peckitt's bill for and of Robert Pranker's engraving of the window are printed in 'William Peckitt, Glass-painter', 57, pl. xxviii.
[4] Fellow of New College, 1761–76, Bishop of Norwich, 1805–37.

recommend the same caution wch. I took of making him produce his figures to some good judges of drawing, who might select from them such as should be most suitable to your design, & who should be capable of pointing out & directing any alterations necessary to be made in them. Mr. Peckitt has a good taste in forming Gothick niches for his figures, & arranging the proper ornaments for them. If your windows are large & you intend to fill them with History pieces, you must be at the expence of a good drawing, wch. I think would be more accurate if it was done of the same size with the intended picture. It will not require a finished drawing, but only an outline slightly shaded in its proper colours as a direction for his work. In this as well as the other case, Mr Peckitt should be consulted, though not employed as draughtsman. It would be right to send him the exact form & size of your windows. You might hear what he has to say about the figures & he will send them to you no doubt, for your inspection & choice. If there is any other particular in which I can be of use to the Gentlemen of the Society they may at all times freely command my service; & as I propose to stay a day or two at Oxford in my way to town abt the 20th. of next month, I will take the opportunity of discussing this point wth you personally. In the meantime give me leave to subscribe myself S^{r.}

Your Most Obed^t
Humble Servt
Jer Milles[1]

Peckitt submitted a revised estimate of cost. It may be inferred from his second letter that the College complained that it was too high and pointed out that he no longer offered to take the old glass in part exchange for his new windows. Peckitt then sent a letter to the Dean of Exeter, 'the chief intent of which', as the Dean remarked to the Warden, 'seems to be a justification of himself wth. respect to the price demanded for his work'. The ensuing correspondence is concerned with the choice of an artist to draw the figures for Peckitt. Biagio Rebecca was selected and he was asked to take as his subjects the patriarchs and prophets in the ante-chapel. His coloured drawing of the figures is preserved in the College.[2] Rebecca was an Italian by descent, but was born in England. He was employed as a decorative artist at Windsor castle and elsewhere. He died in London in 1808.[3]

William Peckitt to the Warden of New College

Rev^d. Sir,

I was Favoured with your Letter of the 23^d Dec^r, and have considerd on its Importance; accordingly have calculated the Expense: for executing

---

[1] CD. 54.   [2] It is reproduced in 'William Peckitt, Glass-painter', pl. xxx.
[3] *Bryan's Dictionary of Painters and Engravers*, ed. G. C. Williamson, London, 1904, iv. 202; *Dictionary of National Biography*, xlvii. 367.

in the most improved manner, in Figures, Three of the Windows on the North side of the inner Chapel of New College. (Each of which windows consists of Eight larger Devisions, and each of these measure I believe about Twenty Eight square feet.) My price for distinct Figures of about six Feet high, in Niches, with Pedestals, and Pinnacle Work (as, after the same Gothick Design of those at present in the Chapel) one part with the other, is One Guinea p^r foot square. Within this charge I will be at the expence of the Outlines of the Figures: that you may fix upon. But if you approve to git these drawn, I will allow for each Figure (in Outlines Only if necessary, but correctly done) One Guinea. The other necessary drawings of the Ornaments above and below them I have by me allready, from those in the Chapel.

The considerable improvements I hove made since I painted your Great West Window, afford Finer productions but require more labour in the Execution: so that the advance in the price from what those Figures paid, is necessarily required.

If You approve of these Windows to be done in wrought Mosaic as the patterns I sent the late Warden, the price must be one Guinea p^r· foot square.

If the Three Windows are to be erected at one time the expence of Cases, and Carriage of them to Oxford will cost you about Twelve pounds. And the charge of one journey, with the value of my time in comeing to Oxford to see that the same are properly placed (which likely will take up One Month, not to exceed) must be Thirty Guineas. The expence of erecting the scafolding, and the Glass, must be defray'd by the Gentlemen of the Society.

The small Figures in the lesser Divisions the upper part of the windows I believe need not be done anew, but will answer tolerably well; (except you chuse) Only may be taken down, cleaned, and new leaded, and so put again: This may be done at Oxford by your Glaziers after I come there, and before the new part is put up.

These are my lowest Terms in General: But in consideration of Three of the Windows You are pleased to mention being Ordered, and Erected togeather, I will out of their Charge, return Fifty Pounds.

No part of the Money will be required to be advanced, till the Glass arives at Oxford.

I am;

Rev^d. Sir

Your Very Obedient servant

W^m. Peckitt.

York

Jan^y· 2^d. 1772

The shape of the Top (from the spring of its Arch) of one of the larger Devisions must be taken in Paper; with the exact Height, and wedth, marked down on the same, and where the Iron barrs in general intersect, allowing for the Rabate; and then tried to all the others, if they are alike: If in thin paper, may be sent me in a Letter.

On the outside of the letter is written:

One Guinea per foot square
Carriage	12– 0–0
Journeys	31–10–0

Suppose each Window will contain 224 Feet

224 Ft at 1–1–0 per ft £235– 4–0	
Carriage	4– 0–0
Journey	10–10–0
	249–14–0

Promise to return 50£ on acc^{nt}. of 3 Windows being order'd together
Therefore

From	249–14–0
Deduct	16–13–4
Ballance	233– 0–8[1]

William Peckitt to the Warden of New College

York Feby. 7. 1772

Revd Sir.

I am favour'd with Yours. My proposals to you is but Reasonable, and not more then what I have receivd some time ago, and even at present have for the like manner of work in large Designs in hand; for in Truth, and the reasons in my former Letter, they are necessarily required. The Dean of Exeter paid me within Two shillings p^r· foot squ$^{e·}$ of my charge to you, near five years ago: at the same time the Window at Oriel College paid one guinea p^r. foot squ$^{e·}$, and £20 for my journey to see the same erected: and this charge is considerably less then was those of Mr Price in his time; since then there is double advance on allmost every necessary article: but I am willing to promote the Art, and therefore, make my prices in a medium way: not doubting but give satisfaction by the works I according produce.

The painted Cartoons you are pleased to mention (being 13) I forwarded to you at Oxford, by the London waggon this day: most part of these the Dean of Exeter show^d· to Mr Ramsey for his oppinion, and was approved; but they are not large enough by one Foot in Height for your windows: notwithstanding inlarged Outlines may be taken from them, if judged proper; as I am apprehensive the same subjects that are allready in the windows You intend to have contrived, but after better Designs. These, or some of them with a little alteration may answer that purpose. I have allso inclosed with them a small Design of Moses & Aaron from which two large Figures might be taken if necessary.

As these windows was mentioned to me by the late Warden to be painted anew at some convenient time, I accordingly took particular notice of their sittuation and manner; and likewise a drawing on paper

[1] CD. 55.

of the full size of one of the Figures, etc. from the opposite side windows; so that I have a sufficient idea: remains only the Exact dimensions as in my former Letter, which your Glazier might readily take, and save my comeing over: Unless You had rather chuse I should wait on You.

If Your Orders should engage me soon, I will propose (God permitt) to execute & erect the Three Windows of Aprill or May 1774.

I cannot recommend to you the joining New work to the Old, as These have neither strength of Colour nor shade to answer Those. for on such wise, we should not receive Credit: neither could I afford for this price the Figures only.

I am very indifferant of purchaceing the Old Glass; for that which I took out of the Great West Window I could not dispose of readily after it was taken down: But I would Recommend, when you have concluded on haveing new windows, to advertize in the London papers of your intention of disposeing of the three Old Ones, (saveing the Crocket Lights) to be Deliverd and Removed at the time the new ones are erected: by that means in all probability you might have a greater price for them then I would care to venture. Notwithstanding, at that time if they are not sold, will allow for them £20; if you should approve.

I am,
Rev^d. Sir,
With Due Respect,
Your Very Obedient Servant
W^m. Peckitt.[1]

William Peckitt to the Dean of Exeter

York March 8. 1772

Revd Sir,

I have great pleasure on finding that the Warden of New College advises with you on the subjects of their intended new windows. My price that I propose to the Warden for them is but reasonable; I considering the largeness of the Work, only charge one Guinea p^r. foot sq^r., out of which I return £50, to defray the expences of the carriage of the Glass, and my journey to see it properly erected etc. besides paying for the Cartoons. You please to be remembered you paid me for your Figures at Exeter with their ornamental-work which has less in them then those at New College; within 2^shill. p^r. foot sq^r. (including the two Guineas each you allow^d. me additional) of this price I have proposed to the Warden; and truely considering all the differant works of your window, I am greatly perswaded you paid me near, if not equal to this charge: if not so, my improvements reasonably should intitle me to it.

My Cartoons with you are very right patterns to extract from, if suteing the Figures intended; but enlarged outlines must be drawn from them, full six feet high, as you will please to see by the enclosed draught. The person I intended to employ is a Liminer of York who draws very well, and who with my directions I doubted not of hoveing good out-

[1] CD. 56.

lines, sufficient for my use, after proper advice from the Warden what Figures to be done. The tinting of the colours (for perticular reasons in the art) must be left to my disposeing: not but if you had rather approve, I shall gladly receive cartoons so finished as you please to have done: which if you think good to hove executed in London, I allow One Guinea for each original Figure, and half a Guinea each for a copy from my own: which is I believe what they would cost me if done here. you probably have along with those cartoons two small Figures of Moses & Aaron if such figures as these should be wanted.

If I knew what Figures the Warden intends to have done, I might collect in due time other good designs to draw from.

Most part of the tabernacle work belonging to the Figures on the S. side of the Chappel was old Glass (repaird and new leaded by Mr Price) of very faint colours & shades, not properly agreeing with new work. The Warden I suppose cannot mean for the new ones on the N. side to correspond with those in Colour, but only in Design, for my proposals are to execute all the parts of the work alike in the Best manner.

The designs for the windows at Audley End being two small sketches in watercolours, and outlines drawn at large by Mr Rebens (an assistant to Mr Cepriani) and are done very correct. The first of these windows was erected this last summer; Sir J. G. Griffin exprest himself exceedingly pleased with it. The other I am now in hand with.

I am sorry Mr Cepriani is not my friend, I do not know the reason why; I was never in his company but once, when I waited on him by the desire of the Bishop of Peterborough, and he seem to behove to me extreamly civil.[1]

I have not as yit receiv'd any answer from the Dean of Chichester.

I have finished for Mr Horace Walpole and sent to Strawberry Hill Ten Lights or panes of Glass with Gothic Borders and shields of double Arms of intermarriages of his Family.

I desire to acqueest with the Gentlemen of the College in Giveing you Thanks, for your Favour intended us.

And Am

Rev^d. Sir

With Dutyfull Respect

Your most Obliged Servant

W^m. Peckitt.

P.S. I hove some hopes of being in London in May next, and will beg the freedom to wait of you.[2]

---

[1] Giovanni Battista Cipriani, painter and etcher, was born at Florence in 1727 and came to England in 1755. He was one of the foundation members of the Royal Academy in 1768. He died at Hammersmith in 1785 and was buried in the Chelsea burial-ground, Bartolozzi erecting a monument to his memory. In 1774–5 he and Peckitt combined to produce an extraordinary window to the honour of Sir Isaac Newton for the library of Trinity College, Cambridge. *Bryan's Dictionary of Painters and Engravers*, i. 297: Willis and Clarke, *Architectural History of the University of Cambridge and the Colleges of Cambridge and Eton*, ii. 547.   [2] CD. 57.

The Dean of Exeter to the Warden of New College

Grosv[r]. Street March 18. 1772

Rev[d]. S[r].

Whilst I was out of toun last week the enclosed letter & draught came from Mr Peckitt; the chief intent of which seems to be a justification of himself wth. respect to the price demanded for his work. I cannot make any accurate comparison between the price of our window & yours, nor indeed is it necessary because Mr P. founds his demand on the improvements he has made in his art.

I have talked wth. Mr Wale on the subject of the Cartoons.[1] He offer'd to draw them for a little more than a guinea perhaps for a guinea and a half each, but I am still at a loss for some good original drawings from which these Cartoons may be equid [sic]. If Mr Pecket allows a guinea for each Cartoon, the additional price paid to Wale or any other artist will not be considerable; but indeed I am doubtfull whether Wale is artist enough to draw the Cartoons as well as we could wish to have them, though I have no doubt of his executing them better than any draughtsman whom Mr Peckitt may have at York. I agree wth. Mr Peckitt that the new work need not be so faint & thin colourd glass as the South side merely to preserve an uniformity. As Pecket will be in toun in May, I think much might be done in promoting this work, if you were in toun at the same time. If in the meantime you think proper I can employ Wale to make a couple of Cartoons of two of the most expressive characters in your N windows & see how he succeeds in them, but by the List in your letter which I have just now the favour of receiving, there seem to be very few who have any characteristical distinction. The figures should certainly be of the same dimensions wth those of the South side. The removal of the upright barrs will be very useful, the horizontal ones will be placed according to Mr Peckitt's directions, to whom I shall write soon in answer to his letter. I think you will be embarassed for criterias to distinguish so many Patriarchs Prophets etc. If I can be of further use to you be pleased freely to command the services of

Rev[d.] S[r.]
Your Most Obed[t.]
Humble Serv[t.]
Jer Milles.[2]

The Dean of Exeter to the Warden of New College

Grosvenor Street Ap 10th 1772

Rev[d] S[r].

I have made it my business for some time past to look out for a draughtsman to execute your Cartoons. I was recommended to a young

[1] Samuel Wale practised decorative painting in the style of Francis Hayman. He was chosen a foundation member of the Royal Academy and became 'professor of perspective' and, later, librarian. He died in 1786. *Bryan's Dictionary of Painters and Engravers*, v. 328–9. [2] CD. 58.

man lately come from Rome & who had studied there for some years. His name is Blackburn. I shewd him as a specimen those of Mr Peckitt; & asked what he would expect for doing some in the same stile. He demanded 10 guineas a piece, said that he was ambitious of having his works known to the publick, & offerd to do one or two for me at a less price, but it was in vain to think of engaging him on any reasonable terms. I then applied to Mr Wale who had offerd to make a Cartoon in chalk for a guinea or a guinea & half. I desired him to give me a sketch of John the Baptist as one of the most characteristical ones in the number. He brought me the enclosed, by which you will judge, as I do, that he is by no means capable of executing such a work. I must therefore put him off with some excuses, & pay him a croun for the attempt, if you approve of it. But where to apply next I am at a loss: There appear at present to me only two methods to be pursued; either to order Peckitt to send a Cartoon to toun drawn by his man for the approbation of Judges, or else to have the drapery of the figures in your North windows traced over, on Cartoons, which may supply you wth. better outlines & more graceful attitudes than you will be able to procure elsewhere, especially as it will be so difficult to vary & characterise the several Patriarchs & Prophets of the Old Testament. I do not recollect what the merit is of your present figures: they are more likely to be deficient in colouring than in design.

I shall stay in toun till May, till which time I shall be glad to render you & the College any service that may be wanted in this city. The present Cartoons as far as they go should undoubtedly be used You will not find better, the rest must be supplied as well as you can. I forget the breadth of your niches. I think they are more than 2 feet but should be glad to have that ascertained I mean the clear room for the figure exclusive of the Gothick pillars on each side.

I am Rev^d S^r

Your Most Obedient

Humble Servant

Jer. Milles

You may observe that Wale has given John the Baptist short garments; I would recommend all the figures in your window to be dressed in long flowing garments which add great dignity to them. I have scrawled out some lines on the back part of Mr Wales figure to shew the different effect of long garments, but as I am totally ignorant in design I only send it to shew the different effect of the garments.[1]

Note from the Dean of Exeter

(Undated)

Mr Warden is desired to procure a List of the figures in the N side Windows of the Chappel distinguishing the orders in wch. they are arranged in each window, & to mark any Kings or Prophets who may

[1] CD. 59.

be represented in the S. windows, that they may not appear again in any of the new painting. To measure accurately the length of the figures on the N & S windows & to judge whether the difference of 6 inches would be very observable between each side of the Chappel. To observe whether the upright barrs can easily be taken out & at what distance the cross barrs are from each other & how they stand in respect to the figures.[1]

Biagio Rebecca to the Warden of New College

London 9th June 1772.

Sir,

Before I sent the drawings to Oxford I examined them with the utmost attention & also took the opinion of an eminent Painter who favor'd me with his approbation of them—I hope they are no way deficient in correctness! & any other alteration may be easily made in the figures already finish'd; & to prevent the necessity of it in the others, I have sent a sketch of them which if you approve I shall endeavor to finish as correctly as possible; but it will be impossible for me to begin them again after the large drawings are done, at the small price I have engag'd for.

As I am going out of town very soon, shall beg the favor of a speedy answer with a return of the drawing to

Sir Y[r.] most Obed[t.] Hble Serv[t.]

Biagio Rebecca.

Please to direct to me at S[r] Jn[o] Griffins, New Burlington Street.[2]

On the back of this letter, in the handwriting of Dr. Oglander, Warden, 1768–94:

'Judah—King
Adam from Raphael leaving Paradise
Abraham & Isaac, bad figures
More feet & legs'

The Dean of Exeter to the Warden of New College

Deanery Exeter
Aug 3[d]. 1772

S[r].

Mr Rebecca thinking that I was in London sent me the enclosed drawing of Adam & Eve from Raphael, they may be properly expressive of the fall in an Historical painting, but as single figures, in windows, I see no propriety in describing them in the manner that Raphael has expressd. you will be pleased to signify your opinion to Mr Rebecca

[1] CD. 110. [2] CD. 60.

at Audley end you may put y^r letter under care to Sr John Griffin at Audley end near Saffron Walden.

I write in great haste & have only time to subscribe myself

Dear S^r

Y^r Most Faithfull

& Obed^t Servant

Jer. Milles

Adam & Eve should be represented in these windows as the common Parents of the other figures, not as the authors of their misery.[1]

Peckitt got to work on the three windows in the second half of 1772 and received the first payment for his work in January, 1773:

William Peckitt's Receipt

York Jany 7th 1773.

Receiv^d of the Rev^d the Warden & Fellows of the Society of New College Oxford the sum of eighty pounds in part, for Figures stain'd in Glass now here in hand with, and to be erected in their Chapel.

£80. 0. 0.

p^r me William Peckitt[2]

William Peckitt to the Bursars of New College

Sir

I have just been Favour'd with yours, with a Draught enclosed on Messrs Child & Com^y for £80, agreeable to my Receipt enclosed in my former Letter, of the 7th Inst: and am much obliged to You.

I have almost compleated my second Figure in Glass, and which as soon as finished, with the Former, will forward to New College agreeable to Desire.

I am

Sir

your most obliged servant

Wm Peckitt

York Jany 30. 1773[3]

The College found that Peckitt's glass, especially the canopy-work, was not to its liking. An attempt was made to restrict his work to two windows, which were to be put in place before the third window was begun. Peckitt was distrustful of this plan and insisted that the College should keep its side of the bargain. The three windows were completed. Peckitt received £420 in October, 1774. He asked that he might have the balance (£217)

[1] CD. 61.   [2] CD. 61^A.   [3] CD. 61^B.

at Christmas. After repeated requests and a complaint from the College that his charges were 'enormous', he received it in June 1775.

Order Book of the Warden and Thirteen[1]

Ordered Dec[r.] 1773
That Mr Thorpe enter into a Correspondence with Mr Peckitt of York on the subject of the Chapel Windows & that he be empowered to put a stop to the work at his discretion till he shall have laid before the thirteen the state of the work & the substance of his Correspondence.

J. H. Thorpe to William Peckitt

Salisbury. Dec[r.] 31st 1773

Sir
Being authoriz'd by the Society of N. College (of w[ch]. I am a member) to correspond with you on the subject of their intended windows, I beg the favour of you to communicate to me the exact state of the several distinct parts of the work, so far as they are finished or begun. That is, I would know how many of the figures are compleated, & whether or not you have made any preparations for the Niches in w[ch]. they are to stand. I cannot help expressing my own hopes that you may not yet have made any progress in the latter; & in case you have not, desire you still to desist for the present, upon reasons of w[ch]. you shall be inform'd in my next letter. In the meantime I expect y[r] answer

       & Am Sir
         Yr etc
           J. Thorpe[2]

William Peckitt to J. H. Thorpe

Sir.
Yisterday I was Honour'd with your Letter of the 1st Inst. The Figures in Glass for the windows of the Chapel of New-College are in much forwardance; perticularly those, of Adam, Eve, Seth, Enoch, Mathusalah, Noah, Abraham, Isaac, Baruch, Hosea, Daniel, Ezekiel, Joel, Amos, Obediah, Jonah are allready compleated: The upper lights, containing the corresponding heads & pinnacle work of the Niches wherein these Figures stand, are likewise finished; excepting two of them, which are now in hand, and will be finished in better than a week. Four of the pedestals for under these Figures are compleated; and four more are allso immediately in hand with.

The remaining Figures, with their corresponding Lights are under such prepairation that I doubt no part can be delay'd, but will require

---

1 'The Warden and Thirteen (Seniors)' was the name given to the ordinary governing body of the College.
2 CD. 62.

to be proceeded with respectively till the whole are compleated: which I imagine will be by the end of the summer.

Any Instruction you may think necessary, I shall be glad to receive

I am,

Sir

With Due Respect

Your Most Obedient Servant

W^m. Peckitt

York

Jany 8th 1774.[1]

J. H. Thorpe to William Peckitt

Sir.   New College, Oxford. Ap^l. 2^d. 1774.

I have submitted to the society your letter of the 8th. of Jany. last; by wch they understand that sixteen figures wch. you have nam'd together with the Niches & corresponding parts are in such a state of forwardness as to admit of no delay. These will form two Windows wch. they desire to see compleated that they may judge of their effect before you take any steps towards proceeding on a third. I am sorry to remark that the shrine-work of your Niches is not of that pure gothic I could wish, bearing too much resemblance to those grotesque designs wch. should never be admitted into any serious compositions. I beg the favor of a line expressing the state & progress of your work, & am Sir

Y^r. most Ob^t.

J. H. Thorpe.[2]

William Peckitt to the Warden of New College

Rev^d. Sir.

It may be necessary to acquaint you that the Windows I have in hand for the Chapel of New College proceed on in the execution regularly; the two first Windows are compleated, and some part of the third, and which I hope will allso be finished in about five or six months. As the several removals of the Cases with the Glass to and by the common Waggons would render it so very precarious, and as the weight will be considerable, I purpose to send them from York to New College in a carriage by themselfs, conducted by two proper men; by which means there will be less apprehension of damage & disappointment: I cannot precisely judge wheather this method of conveyance may exceed the expence that I mention'd, with my proposals, but if it shou'd, I will answer to what addition may be thought agreeable by the Gentlemen of the Society.

I am,

Rev^d. Sir

With Due Respect

Your very Obedient Servant

W^m. Peckitt.

York April 7th. 1774.

[1] CD. 63.   [2] CD. 64.

D

Rev^d. Sir,

Just the moment before I sealed this Letter, I received one from Mr Thorp, wishing to have two of the Windows erected, before I proceed further: I cannot concur with this; as some part of the Third is quite finished, other parts of it are painted, and not pass^d. the Fire; so that it is imposible I should leave this work till compleated: besides I have regulated my time with other Gentlemen in such a manner that it could not be done with convenience. As to the work in General, I doubt not in the least of it giveing satisfaction; and corresponding tho: in a regular manner, with those opposit.[1]

William Peckitt's Bill

Wm Peckitt's Bill. 1774.

Painted & Stained in Glass for the Chapel of New College Oxford, September 1774.   p^r. Willm. Peckitt.

	£ s. d.
Twenty four Figures of Patriarks and Prophets. (Namely. Adam, Eve, Seth, Enoch, Mathusalah, Noah, Abraham, Isaac, Jacob, Judah, Moses, Aaron, Baruch, Hosea, Daniel, Ezekiel, Joel, Amos, Obediah, Jonah, Micah, Nahum, Habakkuk, Zephaniah) with their ornamental work of Canopys & Pedistals. Measuring in All 678 square feet at One Guinea p^r. Foot Square	711–18–0
Expence of Post Chaise to & from Oxford for M^r. Rebecca and self to take Observations on the Windows, in May 1772	6 – 6–0
My present journey to superintend the Erecting of Three Windows	31–10–0
Paid for the Carriage of the Glass to New College	13–16–0
Paid for eleven Cases, etc for the conveying of the Glass	4 – 0–0
	767–10–0
Receiv^d. in part, as by Receipt	80–00–0
To be returned in consiquence of these three Windows being Order^d. & Erected at one time	50–00–0
	£637–10–0[2]

William Peckitt to J. H. Thorpe

York.   29 Octo^r. 1774

Rev^d. Sir

I was Favour^d. with Yours Yesterday.

In regard to the Validity of my Bill, you will please to look over my Proposals to the Warden, wherein you will find that out of the One

[1] CD. 65.   [2] CD. 66.

Guinea p^r. foot sq^r. for the Glass. I was to find the drawings & cartoons; The Society to pay the Expence of cases, carriage, my journey, (to superintend the putting up of the Glass) and erecting the windows; And on provision three windows was ordred & erected at one time, I would out of my Charge, return £50 towards defraying those Expences. In my Letter to the Dean of Exeter, that you are pleased to mention, I explained to him the reasonableness of that charge; of which I did not mean to abate; In those words in perticular, I only charge One Guinea p^r foot square, out of which I allow £50, to defray Expences etc.

I shall be much Obliged to You, You please to send me a Draught for £420, Payable to Me or Order 12 days after Date; upon your own Banker in London, Or if equaly convenient to you on Messrs. Lee Ayton & Co. Bankers in Lombard Street London. On my receiving the said Bill on Saturday or Sunday the 5th. or 6th. of Novr. next, will forward my Receipt for the same to arive at Oxford by the 9th. or 10th., following; On failour of such, it would not be improper You would please to Order the stop of payment. The remaining £217–10–0 being to be remitted to me at Xmas will be agreeable.

I am Rev^d. Sir
With Due Respect
Your Very Humble servant
W^m. Peckitt

On Tuesday next I hope to forward to Mr Bolton your Glazier at Oxford, two panes of Glass that will then be finished, to replace those in the top and pedestal of one of the Figures, that was broke in the Carriage.[1]

William Peckitt to the Warden of New College

York Novr. 1774

Rev^d. Sir.

By yesterday's Post the Favour of Your Draught on Hen: Hoare Esqr. & Co for £420. is come safe to hand: and agreeable as You are pleased to desire, will as soon as the Cash is receivd send you a proper Receipt for the same

I am Rev^d. Sir
With Due Respect
Your Very Obedient servant,
W^m. Peckitt

Last week I forwarded a small Case to Mr Bolton your Glazier with some panes of Glass, one to replace a broken one in the new window, a new Head for the Figure of the V. Mary; which I hope will look more Gracefull, and a more correct Name, for under the same Figure.[2]

[1] CD. 67. [2] CD. 68.

William Peckitt's Receipt

York Nov[r] 26. 1774

Receiv[d]. of the Rev[d]. the Warden and Fellows of New College in Oxford Four Hundred and Twenty Pounds, in part, for the three new painted Windows erected in their Chapel, September last.

p[r]. Me. William Peckitt.[1]

William Peckitt to the Warden of New College

York Jan[y] 16. 1775

Rev[d]. Sir.

I will take it extreamly kind you will please to favour me with the remittance of the remaining part of my Note for the new windows, (by Draught on your Banker as before) as M[r]. Thorpe was pleased to mention I should receive by this time.

I hope Mr Bolton hath received some days ago a second case, containing two panes of Glass to replace those that were broke; and I am extreamly sorry for the accidents in the former cases. The Virgin's Head I will take a future opportunity to execute and convey when I think I can do it with safety.

I am,
Rev[d]. Sir
With Due Respect
Your Very Obliged Servant
W[m] Peckitt.[2]

William Peckitt to the Warden of New College

York Jan[y]. 31 1775

Rev[d]. Sir.

I took the Freedom to wright to you fifteen days ago, on requesting the Favour of a Draught for the remainder of my note; haveing receivd no answer, I am dubious wheather the same came to hand, or if you have wrote, I thought this requisit to acquaint you that I have not yit receivd it.

I am, Rev[d]. Sir
With Due Respect
Your very Obliged Servant
W[m]. Peckitt.[3]

William Peckitt to W. Cooke

Rev[d]. Sir.

I received your Letter of the 20th. inst. and perceave you are under some mistake therein, in regard to my Terms; which I sent by Letter to the Society, and was agreed on by Orders given for the work; and from

[1] CD. 69.   [2] CD. 70.   [3] CD. 71.

which I do not deviate: That is One Guinea p^r. foot square for the paintings: out of which, in case three windows was ordered & erected at one time, I agreed to allow £50 (which is more then the two articles you are pleased to mention, and which you will find on inspecting my Bill, is deducted from the £711–18^s–0^d) towards the following exclucive expences, of which the Society was also to defray; namely the Cases, Carriage, Erecting the Glass, and 30 guineas for my journey & attendance at New College, on the proper erecting the same.

The 6 guineas charged to the society, was the expences of my journey to Oxford with M^r. Rebecca to take dimensions of the windows by the Warden's desire.

As to the price, I am sorry you call it enormous: I rather think it is not rightly understood. The expences of study & experiments, to the acquireing and perfecting of this Art, reasonably would have allow^d. me to have charged more: but on consideration of your Order, and in Respect to the College, who seems to Glory in productions of this kind, I acted consistantly for several works of the same kind painted before those for You, and perticularly some at present in hand, allows me much greater price.

I am,
Rev^d. Sir.
Your very Humble servant.
W^m. Peckitt

York
Feb. 24. 1775[1]

William Peckitt to W. Cooke

Rev^d. Sir.

Some time ago I receiv'd a Letter from You relateing to my Note for the new windows in Your Chapel New College; and agreeable to your desire I immediately return^d. you my answer to the same: but haveing not been favoured with your remittance, as Mr Thorpe, and you was pleased to inform me should be some time since; I humbly take the freedom to hope for your Draught on your Banker in London for the remaining £217–10^s–0^d will greatly oblige

Rev^d. Sir
Your very Humble servant
W^m. Peckitt.

York
April 25. 1775.[2]

Extract from Building Fund Book 1767–97

1775. 'June 9 Mr Peckitt in full for the Chapell Windows £217–0–0'

As has already been said, the College received a legacy of £100 from Henry Coker for the glazing of the two westernmost windows on the north side of the choir. His two brothers also

[1] CD. 73.   [2] CD. 72.

made benefactions for the new windows. John Coker, Fellow of New College 1717–42, who died in 1767, bequeathed £100, and Thomas Coker, Fellow of New College 1724–45, bequeathed £150:

> 1769 'Aprill 4th. Of the Revd Mr Coker a 2nd legacy given by the late J. Coker Esq. towards putting up two new Windows in the Chapel ... ... £100'
> 1774 'Sept 18. Rev. T. Coker for a window ... ... £150'[1]

John Taylor, Fellow of New College, 1726–50, and of Winchester College, gave £100 'towards a new Chapel window' in 1772. He bequeathed a further £200 'towards the Chapel windows'. The £200 was, with an earlier contribution of £21, put towards the cost of the later glass in the great west window.[2]

The College was left with the original glass from the three windows which Peckitt had filled, and they sought advice about how best to use it. On 30 March 1775, it was decided 'that the man [Mr. Lovegrove of Marlow] who has lately been employed upon the window at All Souls be sent for to give his opinion concerning the Old Glass taken from the Chapel' and on 9 November of the same year Lovegrove, who was a coach-painter at Great Marlow, received 5 guineas 'for his Journey etc concerning the Chappell Windows'.[3] Mr. Lovegrove evidently advised the College to use the glass to fill the southern and western windows of the south aisle of the ante-chapel and to store any surplus glass for subsequent repairs. A glazier named John Taylor was employed:

John Taylor's Bill 1775

'New College Dr. to John Taylor'

Sep. 5. To new Glazing, Cleaning, Cementing a Window in the Ante Chapel made from the Old Glass ...	£23–12–6
do. To 4 feet of Coloured glass from London to make good Deficiencies, but not approvd at 5s per foot ...	1 – 0–0
Dec. 7. To one Window more as per Contract	25 – 0–0
	49–12–6

Recd. 15 of Decr. 1775 of the Revd. Mr Cook
Bursar the contents in full
                                        per John Taylor.

---

[1] Building Chest Account.   [2] See below, p. 50.
[3] College Order Book, 30 March 1775: Building Chest and Livings Consolidated Account, 9 November 1775.

The College next decided that Taylor should take down, re-lead, and re-erect the five other windows of ancient glass in the ante-chapel. He did three windows, probably the western window and the two northern windows in the north aisle. He received £83. 6s. for this in 1776.[1]

At the end of the year the College resolved:

'That after the windows in the Ante Chapel are finished, if in the remaining glass there be any figures or parts of figures tolerably compleat they be leaded and secured, that the remainder be separated according to its colours into parcels and the whole in proper boxes be lodged in the Muniment House for future repairs of the Windows.'[2]

In the following year Taylor dealt with the two remaining windows. He was paid £35 for each window and £4. 12s. 6d. for sorting the glass.[1]

In light 2 in the lower tier of lights in the east window of the north aisle a piece of glass has been scratched with a diamond, *Releaded by W. Curtis of Abingdon 1775*. Another piece of glass, removed from one of the chapel windows, has *Richard Fleming Glazer 1775 Willm Curtice Glazier 1777 (Li)ght Leaded 1777*.[3]

The two easternmost windows on the northern side of the choir remained to be newly glazed. The College decided to seek another glass-painter and another designer. They chose Thomas Jervais to be the glass-painter. He and his brother John, who died in 1804, had practised glass-painting in their native city, Dublin. On the advice of their friends, they later sought a wider scope in England. At the time that he was working for the College, Thomas was living in Margaret Street, Cavendish Square, London. He later moved to Windsor, where he died on 29 August 1799.[4]

The earliest letter concerning the windows is as follows:

Thomas Jervais to the Warden of New College

London. June 26, 1777.

Revd Sir,

I rec^d your favor of 23^d, am happy to find I am thought worthy [of] the employment of so respectable a Society, and hope (unless your expectations are very great) to give Satisfaction.

I have not the least objection to any capital Artist making the designs, but wish to be understood in regard to e'm; Mr. West means (if employ'd) to make accurate paintings after nature, the full-size, which makes the estimate for painting the Glass proportionatly less; if small,

[1] Bursar's Long Book.
[2] Order Book of the Warden and Thirteen, 18 December 1776.
[3] See below, p. 96.
[4] *Dictionary of National Biography*, xxix. 353–4.

or slight Sketches are procur'd, I shou'd have studys to make for all the extremities, and very likely for draperies; so that in that case I cou'd not abide by my present Estimate.

but if any Artist be prefer'd, that wou'd do what Mr. West propos'd, it will be equal to me, as I have no Motive in recommending Mr. West more than an opinion of his excellence in this Stile of design, and I believe wou'd exert himself on the occasion.

I shall esteem it a favor my mentioning Mr. West may not be publish'd, as I shall make enemy's by my seeming partiallity—I wou'd wish the society to bargain for the designs, and I will deduct the sum I mention'd out of my estimate. I will agree to the delivering the glass at New College, excepting the carriage they will be convey'd in, should break down or be overturn'd, in that case it will be less felt by a Society than an individual—in regard to time of executing I cannot tell how to answer, but will engage not to undertake anything of consequence, till they are finish'd—I judge (illness excepted) from the time I receive the first drawing, about eighteen Months or seperatly, each figure in nine weeks. Respecting the payment I expect a power to draw for money in proportion to my estimate as the Work is finish'd, that is, when one compartment is Compleat to be paid forty five guineas if I furnish designs 55—for your security you may have the finish'd work lodg'd to your Appointment and in Case of my death, before the whole is finished, My executor to be paid for all that is compleated and unpaid for—if these proposals are agreeable to the Society, I will sign a Contract as soon as you please—as to the other Window, I imagine we shall not differ about it, if I am happy enough to succeed in the first, if I do not, it will not be for want of Attention.

I am with the greatest respect

Your most Obed[nt] Hum[e] Serv[t]

Thos[s]: Jervais.[1]

This letter shows that the College had proposed to Jervais that he should paint the glass for one window and that if the results were satisfactory he should also fill the other. The College had apparently asked Jervais to suggest an artist who could prepare the cartoons for the windows and it was presumably with its approval that Jervais had spoken to Benjamin West, who was later to succeed Sir Joshua Reynolds as President of the Royal Academy.[2] The College did not accept his recom-

---

[1] CD. 89.

[2] Soon after the New College windows were finished, West, Jervais, and Forrest, a pupil of Jervais, combined to produce a huge representation of the Resurrection for the east window of St. George's Chapel, Windsor (*Court and Private Life in the Time of Queen Charlotte: being the Journals of Mrs. Papendick, Assistant Keeper of the Wardrobe and Reader to Her Majesty*, ed. V. D. Broughton, London, 1887, i. 277–8). It has now been removed. West and Jervais also combined to produce other windows, such as a representation of Samuel and Eli in the Temple, which was sold at Christie's in 1821.

mendation and decided to invite Sir Joshua Reynolds to make the designs. The approach was made through Joseph Warton (1722–1800), Headmaster of Winchester (1766–93) and brother of Thomas Warton the poet. The outcome was successful.

Dr. Warton to the Warden of New College

Wint. June 27 1777

Dear Mr Warden

I shall take care to impart to my friend Sir Joshua Reynolds, with the greatest readiness & pleasure, the subject of the Letter with which you favoured me. And I really cannot sufficiently applaud your Zeal & Attention in carrying on a Scheme so much for the Credit & the ornament of our Sister-College, & which will make your Chappel one of the finest Rooms in Europe. I have begged leave to add my name, with the sum of Twenty Pounds, to those which you communicated to our Warden, & am happy to do any thing in my power to promote so very laudable a Design.

I am, Dear Sir,
Your very faithful
& most obed<sup>t</sup> humble
Servant   Jos. Warton.

Sir Joshua Reynolds to Dr. Warton

London. July 5th, 1777.

Dear Sir

I shall very gladly undertake the making Cartoons for the Windows you mentiond of New College. I shall have an opportunity of seeing the Chapel where they are to be placed the latter end of this month, and shall then be able to form a better judgment of the expence than I can at present, tho' I think it cannot be less than twenty Guineas each figure. If I find your Brother at Oxford he will be able to inform me in regard to what Figures are done, and what to be done and every thing about it. If he should not be there I must beg you to recommend me to the Warden or some of the fellows of the College.

Tomorrow morning I set out for Mr. Rigbys. Garrick went yesterday we shall stay about a week, soon after which I shall set out for Blenheim to Paint the whole Marlborough Family in one Picture. I fear my visit to Winchester must be deferred to the next year when I certainly will make it my way to Devonshire.

I beg my Compliments to the Ladies My sister begs me to add hers.

I am with the greatest respect
your most obliged servant
Joshua Reynolds.

Dr. Warton to the Warden of New College

Wint. July 8. 1777.

Dear Mr. Warden

I here inclose to you the answer I have received from Sir Joshua Reynolds; & thought it much best to send you the Letter itself that you may be enabled to judge of what he says. I am glad he will be so soon at Oxford, that he may himself see the nature of the work, & perhaps he may undertake it on rather lower Terms. You will please, if you should be absent, as my Brother will be, to leave word, who he should call upon at the time of his Visit. I have said I was very sure you would be glad to pay your Compliments to him when he comes, & that you would recommend him to some friend in your absence if that should happen.

I am extremely glad that a Scheme so much for the Honour & Ornament of the College seems to meet with such universal Applause & Encouragement.

I am Dear Sir
your very faithful
& obed[t] serv[t]
Jos. Warton.[1]

Meanwhile an agreement was made with Jervais that he should paint the glass:

'Memorandum of an Agreement made the sixteenth Day of July 1777 Between the Rev[d] John Oglander DD. Warden of S[t] Mary Winton College in Oxford commonly called New College in Oxford on the behalf of himself and the Scholars of the said College of the one part and Thomas Jervais of the other part.

Whereas the said Warden and Scholars are desirous of having a new window of painted Glass put up on the North side of the Chapel in the said College consisting of Eight Compartments and one Figure in each Compartment and propose to have the said Figures drawn and made accurate paintings after nature the full size by some eminent painter and the said Thomas Jervais hath agreed to paint the same on Glass within the time and upon the Terms following (vizt.) The said Thomas Jervais doth hereby promise and agree to paint execute and compleat all the said Figures in Eight Compartments on Glass in the best and most skilfull manner in his power within the space of Eighteen Months from the time he receives the first Drawing and to find and provide the best Glass and all other things necessary for the purpose and to deliver the same at the said College and assist in putting the said Window up in the said Chapel within the time aforesaid. And the said Warden agrees that he and the said Scholars shall find and provide such Drawings or paintings as aforesaid and that one of the said Drawings or

[1] CD. 90–2.

Figures shall be delivered unto the said Thomas Jervais ready for him to proceed with his Work within every two Months after the delivery of the First Figure so as that the said Thomas Jervais shall not be hindered in his said Work and that they will pay unto the said Thomas Jervais upon his compleating and delivering each of the said Figures or Compartments at the said College the Sum of thirty five Guineas in part of payment for the same and the further Sum of ten Guineas each when the whole shall be compleated and delivered and the Window put up and finished. And it is provided and agreed that if the said Thomas Jervais shall happen to die before the whole is compleated that his Exors or Administrators shall be paid for as many of the said Compartments or Figures as shall be compleated and unpaid for at the rate aforesaid (vizt.) Forty five Guineas for each Figure or Compartment upon the delivery thereof at the said College.

    Witness their hands
    Witness   Thos. Jervais'[1]
        Senior

It was evidently decided that the eight main lights of the window should contain female figures representing Religion, the Three Theological Virtues, and the Four Cardinal Virtues. The following letters show that Reynolds had begun work on them by November 1777.

Thomas Jervais to the Warden of New College

London Novr 18th 1777

Revd Sir

    I this day waited on Sr Joshua Reynolds, who shew'd me one of the designs for new College Windows; tis a figure of Religion, very finely compos'd and well calculated for effect, instead of a Niche, he has painted a Sky for the background, we had some conversation on the propriety off it. I told him those already painted were in Niches, and the want of uniformity might be an Objection, he desir'd me to write for your Opinion in regard to e'm. Your speedy determination will much Oblige

                         Yr most Obednt
                         Hume Sert
                         Thos Jervais.

Sir Joshua Reynolds to (?) Robert Pitters[2]

Dear Sir,

    I wish you would be so good as to tell the Gentleman that was with you to day at my house that tho I cannot part with the Picture, I intend

[1] CD. 93.
[2] The letter is addressed to a man named Potter. It was probably intended for Robert Pitters, who became a Fellow of New College in 1756 and died in 1801.

they shall have a Cartoon properly finished with which they may do what they please.

I am with the
greatest respect
Yours
J. Reynolds.

Leicesterfield
  Nov. 10. 1777.[1]

It was at this point that a new plan was suggested and speedily adopted. Peckitt's glass was to be removed from the great west window, and the whole window was to be filled with Reynolds–Jervais glass.

Sir Joshua Reynolds to the Warden of New College

Leicesterfield Dec. 27. 1777.

Sir,
  I am extremely glad to hear the Society have determined to place all our works together in the West window to make one complete whole, instead of being distributed in different parts of the Chapel. In my conversation with Mr. Jervais about it he thought it might be possible to change the Stone work of the window so as to make a principal predominant space in the Centre without which it will be difficult to produce a great effect, as Mr. Jervais is now at Oxford I need add no more. I have allready expressed to him how much I wished this alteration might be practicable.

I am with the greatest respect
your most obedient servant
Joshua Reynolds.[2]

Sir Joshua Reynolds to the Warden of New College

London Jan. 9th. 1778

Dear Sir
  I have inclosed a drawing copied from that which was sent to Mr. Jervais, leaving out what I wish to be removed, by this you will see that I have changed the first intention which regarded the lower tier of the divisions of windows to that of making the large space, in the centre; The advantage the window receives from this change is so apparent at first sight that I need not add the authority and approbation of Sir Wm. Chambers to persuade you to adopt it, indeed not only Sir Willm. but every person to whom I have shewn it approve(s) of the alteration. Mr. T. Warton amongst the rest thinks the beauty of the window will be much improved supposing the Pictures which are occupy(ing) the space out of the question. This change by no means weakens the

---

[1] CD. 94–5.   [2] CD. 95A.

window, the stone pillars which are removed suppo(r)ting only the ornament(s) above which are removed with it.

Supposing this scheme to take place my Idea is to paint in the great space in the centre Christ in the Manger, on the Principle that Corregio has done it in the famous Picture called the Notte, making all the light proceed from Christ, these tricks of the art, as the(y) may be called, seem to be more properly adapted to Glass painting than any other kind. This middle space will be filled with the Virgin, Christ, Joseph, and Angels, the two smaller spaces on each side I shall fill with the shepherds coming to worship, and the seven divisions below filld with the figures of Faith Hope and Charity and the four Cardinal Virtues, which will make a proper Rustic Base or foundation for the support of the Christian Religion upon the whole it appears to me that chance has presented to us materials so well adapted to our purpose, that if we had the whole window of our own invention and contrivance we should not probably have succeeded better.

Mr. Jervais is happy in the thought of having so large a field for the displ(a)y of his Art and I verily believe it will be the first work of this species of Art, that the world has yet exhibited.

I am with the greatest respect
Your most humble
and obedient servant
J. Reynolds.[1]

Correggio's picture 'Night', to which Reynolds refers, was completed in 1534. It is now in Dresden Art Gallery.[2]

The College agreed to the removal of the two middle mullions above the transom and the tracery-work immediately above them, but this stonework was replaced in 1848.[3]

The new plan may have made it necessary to draw up another agreement with Jervais for the figures of the Virtues. The agreement already quoted has this note added to it in pencil:

'Each Figure £47–5–0

This Agreement for one Window on north side of the Chapel was superceded by another for the West Window.'

As will be seen below, Jervais received £50 for each figure except that of 'Charity' for which he received £120. If there was an amended agreement, it is now lost. The draft agreement for painting the glass for the upper part of the window is as follows:

---

[1] F. W. Hilles, *Letters of Sir Joshua Reynolds*, Cambridge, 1929, 59.

[2] For a description and illustrations of the picture see C. Ricci, *Correggio*, London, 1930, 90–3, 171, plates clvii–clviii, cclix.

[3] See below, p. 62.

Dated   July 1780

Mr Peckham presents comp^{ts} to Mr. Blake, begs he will transcribe this Draught on   that Mr. P. may execute it on Saturday the 5th of August

| Harry Peckham Esq for the Warden & Fellows of New College with Mr.   Jervoise | D^{rt} Agreem^t for painting the West Window of New College chappell. |

Mr Peckham desires Mr Jervois will be so obliging as to look over this Draught Mr. P will call on him in a Day or two

Articles of Agreement Indented had made concluded and agreed upon this   Day of July 1780. Between Harry Peckham of the Inner Temple London Esqr. for and on behalf of the Warden and Fellows of New College in the University of Oxford of the one part and Thos Jervais of Margaret Street Cavendish Square of the other part as follows—

In Consideration of the Sum of £700 of lawful Money of Great Britain to be paid by the said Warden and Fellows to the s^{d.} Thos Jer(v)ais at the times and in the manner hereinafter mentioned He the s^{d.} Thos Jervais doth hereby for himself his Exors and Admōrs Covenant and Agree to and with the said Harry Peckham for and on behalf of the said Warden and Fellows that he the said Thos Jervais shall and will on or before Midsummer Day which will be in the Year 1783. Completely finish in painted Glass and Cause to be put up under his Inspection and direction in the Western Window of New College Chapel in Oxford the figures of the Nativity and also on or before Lady Day 1784 two compartments on the left hand side of the Nativity and on or before Christmas Day 1784 two compartments on the right hand of the Nativity according to the Designs of Sir Joshua Reynolds and the Plan or Sketch hereunto annexed the same to be executed to the best of the Abilities Skill and Workmanship *of equal Stile and Workmanship with the Figures of Faith Hope and Charity already Painted on Glass and put up in the said Chapel by* of the said Thos. Jervais Provided the said Sir Joshua Reynolds delivers to the said Thos Jervais two of the said Compartments before the Nativity is dead coloured and the other two Compartments before the first two Compartm^{ts}. are dead Coloured *And the said Thos Jervais also further covēnts and Agrees with the said Warden and Fellows that he the said Thos Jervais shall not or will not whilst the said Work is about and until the same is finished do any other kind of Work* And the said Harry Peckham doth hereby for and on behalf of the same Warden and Fellows Covēnt and Agree to and with the said Thos Jervais his Exors Admōrs and Assigns in manner following that is to say that in Consideration of the Works so agreed to be done by the said Thos. Jervais as aforesaid that the said Warden and Fellows shall and will pay unto the said Thos. Jervais his Exors Admors and Assigns the sum of £700 of lawful Money of Great Britain at the times and in manner following (that is to say) the sum of £40 a Quarter from Christmas next And when the Painting of the Nativity is completed and put up Shall and will make up such payment the sum of £300 and shall and will pay to the s^d. Thos Jervais the further Sum of £200 when and so soon as two of the said Compartments are Completed and put up and the remaining sum of £200, when and so soon as the two other Compartments are Completed and put up.^x And for the true Performance of all and Singular the Matters and things herein before Agreed to be done and performed by the said Thos. Jervais (unless prevented by Sickness) and for Securing the payment of the Money to be paid by the said Warden and Fellows as aforesaid They the said Harry Peckham and Thos. Jervais Do hereby Bind and Oblige themselves to each other and the Heirs Exors and Admors of Each other in the Penal Sum of £500.

In Witness &c.

^xBut if the s^d. Thos. Jervais should die before the Work is completed, the s^d. Warden and Fellows of New College shall take at a fair Valuation all such Work as are *completely done* begun within the Time specified for the completion of such respective parts.

On the back of this draft is written:

| Faith | — 50 | Pd |
| Charity | —120 | |

Journeys	— 8 Gs.
Hope	— 50
Justice	— 50 to be p^d
Prudence	— 50 for immediately

Temperance	50
Fortitude	50
To be finished before Xmas[1]	

Work on the window went forward steadily. The light showing the figure of Faith in the west window has at the bottom Sr *Joshua Reynolds Delin. Thos· Jervais Pinxit 1778.* The figures of Faith, Hope, and Charity seem to have been exhibited in London.[2] They were placed in position at the beginning of September 1779.[3] The *Gazetteer* of 25 April 1780 contained this advertisement:

'Stained glass. Mr. Jervais's exhibition of stained glass is now open at Mr. Pinchbeck's, Cockspur St., bottom of the Haymarket, admittance 1s. . . . two figures of Justice and Prudence (large as life), after

[1] CD. 99. Passages marked * are crossed through in the draft.
[2] See below, p. 54.   [3] See below, p. 53.

Sir Joshua Reynolds, being part of a window for the chapel of New College, Oxford.'[1]

There was delay in painting the glass for the upper part of the window, which seems to have caused the College some concern. Jervais made a spirited reply,

Thomas Jervais to the Warden of New College

London Jan[y] 6: 1783.

Rev[d]. Sir.

Your draught for eighty pounds came safe to hand, for which I am much Oblig'd—you likewise inform me the Society mean not to deviate in the *least* from our Original Agreement, in that case (without undertaking any other bussiness) I may be liable to the forfeiture, unless an Allowance is made for time I waited for the designs, which was upwards of three months for the Nativity, and one month for the Angel, if I recollect right there is an allowance for Illness—You may rely upon it I shall not (willfully) either incur the penalty, or the displeasure of the Society, but really think I cannot fullfill my engagement unless the time I waited for S[r]. Joshua be taken into the account: if I had a coppy of the Article I would endeavour to Adhere to it

I am with much respect

Your Most Obed[nt].

Hum[le]. Ser[t]

Tho[s]. Jervais.[2]

The Nativity scene was exhibited in London in the spring of 1783.[3] On 13 September 1783 the *Reading Mercury and Oxford Gazette* said:

'A few days ago the central piece of the great West Window in New College Chapel was put up. In point of execution it may be pronounced equal to the Seven Figures at the base of the Window. When this Window is completed it will perhaps exhibit the finest specimen of Enamel painting in Europe.'

On 13 August 1785 Jervais sent a receipt for the final payment for his work.[4] Ten days later he wrote the following letter to the Warden:

Thomas Jervais to the Warden of New College

London. Aug[st]. 23[d]. 1785

Rev[d] Sir

I have the Mortification to inform you I have made a blunder in errecting the left side of the window, the portraits should be placed next

[1] A. Graves and W. V. Cronin, *A History of the Works of Sir Joshua Reynolds, P.R.A.*, London, 1899, iii. 1178–9.

[2] CD. 102.   [3] See below, p. 54.   [4] CD. 107.

the Nativity, and the moon light at the extreamity: I was led into this error from the abrupt finishing of my portrait, upon seeing the print at Boydels I perceive S^r. Joshua means the arm should be supposed behind the Mullion. I am in great hope the Scaffold is still up in that case the alteration will be but trivial as I imagine the glass of each will fit either of the Bars without the trouble of moving them. I shall return to Windsor to morrow, and if you think my attendance necessary please to favor me with a line, and I will instantly Obey your summons and am with much respect Yr. Most

Obe^d. Hum^l. Ser^t.
Thos. Jervais.[1]

There is a good description of Reynolds at work upon the designs for the window:

'When he was engaged by the Master and Fellows of the New College to give designs for the west window of the chapel, it was meant that they should be drawings, or cartoons. This he told me; but, calling upon him some time after, I found the figure of *Faith* painted on canvas; the reason for this, as he said, was, that he had been so long in the use of the pallet and brushes, that he found it easier to him to paint them to drawing. "Jervas, the painter on glass", says he "will have a better original to copy; and I suppose persons may be found to purchase my paintings."

When he was employed upon the central part of the window, on his famous "Nativity", I happened to call upon him, when his painting-room presented me with a very singular and pleasing prospect. Three beautiful, young, female children, with their hair dishevelled, were placed under a large mirror which hung angularly over their heads, and from the reflections in this he was painting that charming group of angels which surround the Holy Infant. He had nearly finished this part of his design, and I hardly recollect ever to have had greater pleasure than I then had in beholding and comparing beautiful Nature, both in its reflection and on the canvas. The effect may be imagined, but it cannot be described. The head of the Virgin in this capital picture was first a profile. I told him it appeared to me so very *Correggiesque* that I feared it would be throughout thought too close an imitation of that master. What I then said, whether justly or not I will not presume to say, had so much weight with him, that when I saw the picture the next time the head was altered entirely: part of the retiring cheek was brought forward, and, as he told me, he had got *Mrs. Sheridan* to sit for it to him.'[2]

---

[1] CD. 108.

[2] *Sir Joshua Reynolds' Notes and Observations on Pictures* (being the relevant part of the section entitled 'Anecdotes of Sir Joshua Reynolds, chiefly relative to his manner of colouring'. By W. Mason, the Poet. Copied by the Rev. J. Mitford, from the original manuscript at Aston Rectory in 1851), ed. W. Cotton, London, 1859, 58–9.

E

Mrs. Sheridan also posed for the figure of 'Charity'. The picture was exhibited at the Royal Academy in 1779.[1] There is another version of the group in the Ashmolean Museum, Oxford. The figure of 'Fortitude' is generally said to be a portrait of Elizabeth, third daughter of William Johnson, of Torrington, Devon, and Elizabeth Johnson, who was a sister of Sir Joshua Reynolds.[2] Another tradition says that the model for 'Fortitude' was Lady Dudley and Ward and that at the sale of these pictures in 1821 'Lord Dudley and Ward eagerly competed for the Fortitude, for which his mother sat to Sir Joshua'.[3] It has also been said that the model for 'Prudence' was Elizabeth, daughter of Cadwallader Edwards, of Wexford, and wife of Joseph Palmer, who was Dean of Cashel and a nephew of Sir Joshua Reynolds.[4] It is unlikely, however, that Reynolds was acquainted with her at the time that he was painting this picture. The model for 'Temperance' is supposed to be Frances, sister of Elizabeth Johnson and niece of Reynolds. The model for 'Justice' was Harriet Sophia (ob. 1839), daughter of Colonel William Burrard, of Walhampton, Hants, and wife of Sir Giles Rooke (1743–1808), Fellow of Merton College, Oxford, and Puisne Judge of Common Pleas. Reynolds and Jervais are represented as Shepherds, 'Sir Joshua Reynolds with a staff, kneeling on a rock, and Jervais with his hands uplifted, advancing to the left.'[5]

The cost of the window was met by subscriptions, which were collected by the Warden. There are two subscription books, one in the Warden's handwriting, the other a 'fair copy'.[6] The subscriptions are conveniently summarized in the 'fair copy'.

Warden & Fellows of New College	£582 : 03 : 6
Late Fellows of Do	265 : 0 : 0
Gentlemen Commoners of Do...	293 : 15 : 0
Winchester College	450 : 05 : 0
A Wiccamist	10 : 10 : 0
Interest &c	188 : 15 : 0
	1790. 8. 6[7]

[1] Graves and Cronin, *History of the Works of Sir Joshua Reynolds*, iii. 1185.

[2] S. H. Radcliffe, *Sir Joshua's Nephew, being Letters written, 1769–1778, by a Young Man to his Sisters*, London, 1930, ix; W. R. Hooper, 'An Old Devonshire House and Family', *Devon and Cornwall Notes and Queries*, xix. 342.

[3] M. Roldit, 'The Collection of Pictures of the Earl of Normanton, at Somerley, Hampshire—I. Pictures by Sir Joshua Reynolds', *Burlington Magazine*, ii. 211.

[4] Graves and Cronin, *History of the Works of Sir Joshua Reynolds*, iii. 1187.

[5] Ibid. 1181.   [6] CD. 82–3.

[7] CD. 82–3. The sum of £450. 5s. contributed by Winchester College included John Taylor's benefaction of £221: see above, p. 38.

Jervais received a total sum of £1,544. 15s. for his work and, on 4 January 1778, £6. 6s. 'for his Journey from London to Oxford'. Reynolds received £147 on 16 June 1780, and £84 on 7 May 1785: that is to say, 20 guineas apiece for the Seven Virtues and the four side figures in the upper range.[1] An entry in Reynolds's ledger at the time of the first payment reads 'Mr. Oglander has paid for all the designs of the window at New College, Oxford, except the Great Picture of the Nativity'.[2] He received no payment at all for the great central scene:

Thomas Jervais to the Warden of New College

Windsor   June 28. 1785.

Rev^d. Sir,

I did not receive your favour of the 17th of June, till the 27th., the circumstances you wish to know respecting the Nativity, is to the best of my recolection—viz—I call'd on S^r. Joshua to inform him I was going to Oxford, & to know if he had any commands, during our chat the plan that was adopted occur'd to me—I asked him (if the Society did not object to it) what was his opinion of putting an Historical Subject in the centre of the Window—he seem'd much pleased with the Idea, and commissioned me to inform the Gentlemen (to promote that plan) he would make the design *gratis* and said he had long wish'd to paint an Historical picture and this commission would give him a good pretence. I have nothing to add but that I have the fairest prospect of fulfilling my engagement with you, and am with much respect

Yr Most Obed^t
Hum^l Ser^t
Thos. Jervais

P.S. There will be near 40 Bars wanted for the Glass I shall errect.[3]

Sir Joshua Reynolds to the Warden of New College

Leicesterfield, July 9th 1785

Sir.

Tho I have not the least remembrance of having said to Mr. Jervais that I should not charge anything for the designs for the middle part of the Window, I am very willing to abide by his declaration, especially as you say this proposal principally influenced the College to adopt the plan, such a discourse might very probably pass between Mr. Jervais & myself that rather than such a scheme should not be adopted I would give the designs gratis, but I think I am confident that if I had seriously commissioned him to make such a proposal to the College, I should not

---

[1] Most of the receipts survive: they are CD. 96, 98, 100–2, 104, 107.
[2] Graves and Cronin, *History of the Works of Sir Joshua Reynolds*, iii. 1179.
[3] CD. 105.

have forgot it, the respect due to the Society would have imprinted it on my memory.

Whatever shall be the determination of the College I shall acquiesse with the greatest satisfaction.

I am with great respect

Your most humble

and most obedient servant

Joshua Reynolds.[1]

Reynolds sold his painting of the Nativity (for the use of which the College did not pay him) to the Duke of Rutland for £1,200.[2] It was burnt at Belvoir castle on 26 October 1816. It must have deteriorated very seriously by that time, for in 1788 the paint was flaking off so badly that a napkin had to be placed under it.[3] Reynolds bequeathed the picture of the Angel contemplating the Cross to the third Duke of Portland, in 1792. He bequeathed to his niece Mary Palmer the sum of £100,000, a number of pictures, including eleven paintings for the New College window, and other works of art. In the same year she married the fifth Earl of Inchiquin, who was later created Marquis of Thomond.[4] After her death, the pictures were sold by Christie's, the date of the sale being 19 May 1821.[5] The paintings for the New College windows fetched £7,229. 5s. The Seven Virtues were acquired by the young Lord Normanton for his residence at Somerley at a cost of £5,565. It is said that they attracted him first when he was a boy at Westminster School.[6] Seven years later twice that sum was offered for them on behalf of the king and subsequently the National Gallery offered him three times the purchase price.[4]

The window itself was greeted with a chorus of enthusiastic praise. From this chorus three voices may be picked out. The Revd. James Woodforde, rector of Weston Longeville, Norfolk, and sometime Fellow of New College, contributed 10 guineas towards the cost of the window. In the autumn of 1779 he stopped at Oxford on his way back from Somerset to Norfolk. On 12

---

[1] CD. 106.

[2] C. R. Leslie and T. Taylor, *Life and Times of Sir Joshua Reynolds*, London, 1865, ii. 263.

[3] *The Hamwood Papers of the Ladies of Llangollen and Caroline Hamilton*, ed. J. H. Bell (John Travers), London, 1930, 75.

[4] Roldit, *The Collection of Pictures of the Earl of Normanton, at Somerley, Hampshire*, 211.

[5] The title-page of the sale catalogue and a detailed list of prices and purchasers are printed in Graves and Cronin, *History of the Works of Sir Joshua Reynolds*, iv. 1654, 1662–3.

[6] *The Times*, 8 January 1883.

September he dined, supped, and spent the evening in New College. He says in his diary:

'In the West Window of New Coll: Chapel are three most beautiful emblematical figures of Faith, Hope and Charity, painted on glass. They were done by one Jervase of London, and only put up in the Chapel the last week. No Painting can exceed them I think on glass. The whole of that great West Window is to be painted by him. The design is of Sir Joshua Reynolds's.'[1]

In 1786 the king and queen and others of the royal circle made an expedition to Oxford. Fanny Burney was in attendance. The Duchess of Ancaster commiserated with her upon the length of time that she had to remain standing. Fanny Burney writes, 'The beautiful window of Sir Joshua Reynolds and Mr. Jervis, in New College, would alone have recovered me, had my fatigue been infinitely more serious.'[2]

A more studied praise was accorded to the window and the artists responsible for it by Thomas Warton in 1782.[3] It is a poem entitled *Verses on Sir Joshua Reynolds's Painted Window at New College Oxford*. It was printed for J. Dodsley in Pall Mall and sold by 'Mess. Fletchers at Oxford'.

Sir Joshua Reynolds to Thomas Warton

London May 13th 1782

Dear Sir,

This is the first minute I have had to thank you for the Verses which I had the honour and pleasure of receiving a week ago. It is a bijoux, it is a beautifull little thing, and I think I should have equally admired it, if I had not been so much interested in it as I certainly am; I owe you great obligations for the Sacrifice which you have made, or pretend to have made, to modern Art, I say pretend, for tho' it it [sic] allowed that you like a true Poet feigned marvellously well, and have opposed the two different stiles with the skill of a Connoiseur, yet I may be allowed to entertain some doubts of the sincerity of your conversion, I have no great confidence in the recantation of such an old offender.

It is short, but it is a complete composition; it is a whole, the struggle is I think eminently beautifull—From bliss long felt unwillingly we part ah spare the weakness of a lovers heart!

[1] *The Diary of a Country Parson: the Reverend James Woodforde, 1758–1781*, ed. J. Beresford, London, 1926, i. 264–5.

[2] *The Diary and Letters of Madame D'arblay*, ed. C. Barrett, London, 1893, ii. 144.

[3] Thomas Warton was the brother of Joseph Warton. He was born in 1728. He was educated first by his father and then at Trinity College, Oxford, of which he became a Fellow in 1750. He became Professor of Poetry in 1756 and Poet Laureate in 1785. He published his *History of English Poetry* in 1774–81. He died on 21 May 1790. He sat to Reynolds in January 1784 for his portrait, which is now in Trinity College, Oxford.

It is not much to say that your Verses are by far the best that ever my name was concerned in. I am sorry therefore my name was not hitchd in in the body of the Poem, if the title page should be lost it will appear to be addressed to M^r. Jervais.

> I am Dear Sir
> with the greatest respect
> your most humble
> and obliged servant
> J. Reynolds[1]

When Warton published a second edition of the poem in 1783 he complied with Reynolds's request. A couplet towards the end of the poem was changed from

> 'ARTIST, tis thine, from the broad window's height,
> To add new lustre to religious light:'

to

> 'REYNOLDS, tis thine, from the broad window's height,
> To add new lustre to religious light:'

Another couplet was added earlier in the poem: otherwise no change was made.[2]

The window was a grievous disappointment to Reynolds.[3] It was also sharply criticized by others. On 12 July 1779 Horace Walpole wrote to William Cole:

> 'Mr. Essex agreed with me, that Jarvis's windows for Oxford, after Sir Joshua Reynolds, will not succeed. Most of his colours are opaque, and their great beauty depending on a spot of light for sun or moon, is an imposition. When his paintings are exhibited at Charing Cross, all the rest of the room is darkened to relieve them. That cannot be done at New College; or if done, would be too dark. If there is other light, the effect will be lost.'

He was enthusiastic when he saw the scene of the Nativity in similar circumstances and said in a letter, dated 11 May 1783, to William Mason,

> 'Jarvis's window from Sir Joshua's "Nativity" is glorious. The room being darkened and the sun shining through the transparencies, realizes the illumination that is supposed to be diffused from the glory, and has a magic effect.'

He soon reverted to his original opinion and on 9 September wrote to the Countess of Upper Ossory:

> 'I went to my passion Oxford and saw Sir Joshua's "Nativity". But,

---

[1] British Museum Add. MS. 36526D, f. 14.

[2] Note by R. W. C. in a limited edition of the poem printed by the Oxford University Press in 1930.

[3] *Sir Joshua Reynolds' Notes and Observations on Pictures*, &c., 59.

alas! it is just the reverse of the glorious appearance it made in the dark chamber in Pall Mall. It is too high, the ante-chapel where it is placed is too narrow to see it but fore-shortened, and the washy Virtues round it are so faint and light, that the dark shepherds and chiaroscuro, that are meant to relieve the glory, Child, and angels, obscure the whole. I foresaw long ago, that Jarvis's colours, being many of them not transparent, could not have the effect of old painted glass.'

On 6 October 1785 he repeated the criticism to the Hon. Henry Seymour Conway:

'I dont wonder you was dissapointed with Jarvis's window at New College; I had foretold their miscarriage. The old and the new are as mismatched as an orange and a lemon, and destroy each other; nor is there room enough to retire back and see half of the new; and Sir Joshua's washy Virtues make the "Nativity" a dark spot from the darkness of the shepherds, which happened, as I knew it would, from most of Jarvis's colours not being transparent.'[1]

The Hon. John Byng, afterwards fifth Lord Torrington, thus described the glass, which he probably saw in 1781–2:

'The new Windows of New College are at present the Admiration of Travellers by being the University Boast. Now I am sorry to dissent from this Run of fine taste and would hate to think myself peevish or fastidious; yet I must own I preferred the Old high-coloured Paintings, and their strong, steady Shade, to these new and elegant-esteemed Compositions; and to speak my mind, These twisting emblematical Figures appear to me half-dressed languishing Harlots; No doubt, but that Men of Skill have been consulted, who determined them to be of the Collegiate and Gothic taste, else they never have been introduced into this beautiful old Chapel. My Bolt is shot! Remarks will be made by Travellers, and people should judge for themselves: My Opinions may selldom convince, but yet I hope they will selldom mislead.'[2]

In 1790 5 guineas was paid to Jervais 'for giving directions about the West Window'.[3] There is no clue to the reason for the consultation. In 1798 the College asked his advice about the cleaning of the window. He replied, 'As I was never by profession a Glazier I am not Competent to answer your request respecting the cleaning of your West Window, and the protecting it on the outside.' He advised great caution in the treatment of the window.[4] In a second letter he made it clear that he could not do the work himself and suggested that it should be brushed

---

[1] *The Letters of Horace Walpole, Fourth Earl of Orford*, ed. Mrs. Paget Toynbee, Oxford, 1904–5, x. 450; xii. 447; xiii. 52, 336.
[2] *The Torrington Diaries, 1781–94*, ed. C. B. Andrews, London, 1936, i. 54.
[3] Bursar's Long Book.   [4] Order Book of the Warden and Thirteen.

down with a soft, dry brush or sponged down with a soft sponge and soft water; 'one or both of these methods I think should do'. He added, 'I probably may have recommended more caution than may be found necessary, but think it is a fault on the right side.'[1]

Before leaving all this eighteenth-century activity it must be noticed that the work involved other costs besides the payments to the designers and glass-painters. The following payments are extracted from the Building Chest Account. They are concerned with Price's windows.

June 27th·, 1735.	Paid to Thomas Newman for wiring the same window the sum of five Pounds Eighteen shillings & Sixpence by me.	
	Geo. Cooper Subwarden	
	Ed. Rolle Dean of Div.	
Dec. 16, 1736.	paid to Thomas Newman for wiring the Chappel Window six pound one shilling & sixpence.	
Sept. 10, 1737	For Wiring and putting up the Window Thirteen pounds Eleven shillings & 2 pence	
	J. Cox	
	Hen. Reynell.	
Apr. 6th·, 1738	Repaid to the Ast. Bursar for the porterage for the last Chappell Window	0 – 7 – 6
Dec. 9th·, 1738	To Newman for wiring the Chappell Window	12 – 3 – 0
	Porterage for the Window	0 – 4 – 6
Nov. 21, 1739	Paid for the Wire of the fourth Window	12 – 3 – 0
	also for the Carriage of three Windows	7 – 7 – 0
Dec. 16, 1740	Pd. at the same Time for the Wire & Carriage of the last Window	12 – 12 – 0

The following payments occur in the Bursar's Long Books:

1753	To Bolton Glazier, uti per Bill	04 – 04 – 03
1766	Paid for Carriage of Glass & Porterage of the same	00 – 19 – 0
	To the Porter for Porterage to College	00 – 01 – 0
1773	To Ward (Waggoner) Carriage of a Case of Glass (Windows) for the Chapel	18 – 0
1775	To Mr Newman the remainder of his bill for Lattice to the new windows	76 – 18 – 5[2]

[1] CD. 109.

[2] A separate bill shows that he had already received £50 on account of a total sum of £126. 18s. 'for Seven Hundred & Fifty Feet of Fly Wire Lattice at Three Shillings p. Foot' and 'for One Hundred & Ninety two ft. of Coarser over the Body of the Figures at one Shilling & Sixpence p. Foot'.

1776   To W^m. Teazler Plasterer for pointing the three
windows lately repaired in the Ante-Chapel   4–15–10

To John Randall, Mason, for scaffolding to the
three windows and cutting grooves in the munnions   13–17–8

1777   To Mr Newman as by Bill for new Lattice to one
Window on the south side of the Chapel   20–0–0

To do: for repairing etc the Lattice of another
window, taking it down & putting it up on the North
Side   1–1–0

1778   To Mr Teazler, as by bill for pointing the windows   4–2–0

1779   To Ralph Newman for 314 ft of Lattice to the 2nd
window on the S. Side   20–0–0

To Do: for taking down and putting up again a
Part of the Lattice of the West Window & for Wire
in Ties & Hooks & for an addition of three feet of
Lattice for the same at 9^d pr. foot   9–3

1780   To Newman his bill for wire Lattice to West
Window and the North Window of the Chapel   2–15–0

To Reynolds (Smith) a bill for iron bar work in
the West Window of the Chapel exclusive of £1–12–6
received for old iron   9–6

1783   To R. Newman for putting up the Wire Lattice to
the West Window with an addition of 6 feet of new
Lattice at 6^d. per foot   6–0

To Do: for three hundred & ninety five feet of
strong straight Lattice for the second Window and
two figures of the first on the North side from the
Altar at £20 pr. window the same as in the year 1779   25–0–0

Bolton Glazier, his bill   11–12–2

1785   To John Randall, Mason, for the use of scaffolding to put up the remaining Compartments of the
Western Window & other work   21–5–1

To Bolton Glazier as p^r. Bill   11–7–2½

To J. Green as per Bill for painting 3 times over
in Oil 26 lights in the West Window at 1^s 6^d   1–19–0

To Newman upon Account for Wire Lattice   26–5–0

1786   To Newman for Wire Lattice on account   25–0–0

To Reynolds for ironwork in the West Window   3–4–0

To Newman the remainder of his Bill for wire-
lattice   63–3–6

1790   To Mr Bush his Bill for 96 feet Copper in the
Chapel Window & 12 Gallons of Oil for the Workmen   14–13–4

A collection of New College bills and receipts in the Bodleian Library includes the following:

New Coll. D^r· to R. Newman

1785

Sept the 1st	For taking down Lattice to the West window & puting it up again & Hooks & wire	5 – 0
16	For 316 Feet of Straight Lattice to the four figures to the Window the North side of the Chappel	10 – 0 – 0
Oct the 8	For taking down Lattice to the South Window & puting it up again	0 – 2 – 6
13	For puting up Lattice to the Lardar Windows & hooks	0 – 1 – 0
	For taking down Lattice to the South Window & putting up again & hooks	0 – 1 – 0
1786	For 693 Feet of fine wire Lattice for the use of the West Window of the Chappell at 3^s· per Foot	103 – 19 – 0

£114 – 8 – 6

Rec^d· in part 71 – 5 – 0

Rem^s· 43 – 3 – 6

Rec^d of the Bursars of New College the sum of One Hundred and fourteen pounds eight shillings and sixpence in full of all demaunds for Wire Lattice.

£114 – 8 – 6   Ralph Newman[1]

To Eliz Dyer

1786   March 23rd· To Painting the Wire Lattice for the West Window in the Chapel twice over lead col^r· on both sides 154 yards at 5^d· per yard   £3 – 4 – 2[2]

Among a list of payments in the Warden's Subscription Book for the great west window are these items,

1778	Feb. 10.	Mr Crowe, for Mr Malchair for a Drawing of the Window	1 – 1 – 0
	July 2.	The Bursar, for Mr Malchair	2 – 6
	Decr 28.	Randal for scaffolding	1 – 11 – 0
		Newman for Lattice	5 – 0
1781	Jany 30.	Mr Edgecombe for a Drawing of the Window	1 – 1 – 0
	July 7	for the Carr: of the Glass	5 – 3
1783	Dec.	The Bursar for Mr Bolton	5 – 10 – 6
		for Randall	10 – 5 – 0[3]

---

[1] Bod. MS. Top. Oxon. C. 316, f. 189.   [2] Ibid., f. 167.   [3] CD. 83.

A note concerning the ironwork of the great west window:

'Agust 1783.

The iron work of the grate window in the Chappell w^d 562 pounds which is 500 hundred waight and 2 pounds over at thre pownds and ten shillings a hundred ... 17–11 – 3

Sixteen plugs nuts and screwd Leded in the wall to hold up the outside frame wd 16 pownds ... 10 – 0

Thre men one day a fixing the Iron frame up and two men half a day ... 10 – 0

^11 18–11 – 3

August The 6. Recivd old iron as came out of The grate winder wd 449 pownds which is fower hundred pownd waight and one pownd over at 14 shillings a hundred ... 2–16 – 1½

Recivd of the Warden by Mr Cock ... 5 – 5 – 0

8 – 1 – 1½^11

The College still had on its hands Peckitt's glass from the great west window of the chapel. It was decided that it should be placed in the two easternmost windows on the north side of the choir. This was apparently done in 1788–9. Speaking of these two windows, the 1788 edition of the *Pocket Companion to Oxford* says that they '(when completed) will contain our Saviour, the Virgin Mary, and twelve Apostles'.[2] The 1789 edition omits the words '(when completed) will'.[2] The figures were sufficient to fill all the lights except two. The canopies had to be cut down to fit the lights, which are smaller than those of the west window. The two lights on the left of the lower tier of the easternmost window were left empty until about 1820–1. In the Bursar's Long Book for 1821 there is the entry:

'Term 4to To Mr. Eginton for Chapel
Windows ... ... £219–18–6'[3]

That this sum included the cost of painting the figures of SS. Barnabas and Paul for the two remaining lights is illustrated by the following statement in the 1822 edition of the *Oxford University and City Guide*:

'The window near the altar on the north-side, which was left unfinished, has lately been completed by Mr. Eginton of Birmingham.'[4]

---

[1] CD. 103.
[2] p. 45.
[3] For William Raphael Eginton (1778–1834) see 'Glass-painters of Birmingham', *Journ. British Society of Master Glass-painters*, ii. 69–71.
[4] p. 92.

The 1818 edition of the *Guide* does not contain this statement.[1]

The sum of £219. 18s. 6d. was a very large payment for filling two lights with stained glass. It may be that Eginton was asked to repair some other windows of the chapel at the same time.

As has already been said, the stone mullions and tracery of the west window were replaced in 1848.[2]

In 1845 the Archaeological Institute visited Winchester. The Revd. J. L. Petit read a paper by Charles Winston (1814–64), whose studies in the history of stained glass are still invaluable. In this paper Winston mentions 'two boxes in the cloisters of Winchester College, which are filled with scraps, principally of glass of Wykeham's time, brought from New College Chapel, Oxford'.[3] Winston was told that this glass had been taken from the great west window when Reynolds's glass was put in.[4] This erroneous information led Winston to believe that the window originally contained single figures of saints beneath canopies, for he had examined the glass in the boxes and found such figures, with names, and canopies. He made careful drawings of some of the pieces. These drawings are now in the British Museum. They show: (1–2) thirteenth-century quarries and pieces of glass decorated with acanthus leaves. These fragments must have been used for patching by some glazier; (3) fourteenth-century quarries, probably also used for patching; (4) letters and a crowned catherine wheel from backgrounds; (5) pieces of canopies; (6) a bearded head; (7) a hand; (8) *Sc̄a Ag*, from a light containing St. Agatha or St. Agnes.[5] It is clear that what Winston found at Winchester was at least some of the glass left over from Taylor's work.

It may be remembered that in 1821 the Warden and Fellows of Winchester College decided to restore and repair their glass. It is evident that the Warden and Fellows of New College sent their spare glass for Betton and Evans to use in that work if they wanted to do so. An item in the Winchester accounts reads,

'Carriage of Boxes of Glass from New College for yᵉ Chapel, 3. 11. 6.'[6]

In 1850 the church of Bradford Peverell, Dorset, was being rebuilt. The rector was Henry Blackstone Williams (1812–79). His father, Dr. David Williams, Warden of New College 1840–60,

---

[1] p. 55.   [2] See above, p. 45.
[3] 'A Short Notice of the Painted Glass in Winchester and its Neighbourhood', *Memoirs illustrative of the Art of Glass-painting*, 64.
[4] Ibid. 65.   [5] See above, p. 19.
[6] Winchester College, Bursar's Book, 1812–27, year December, 1822–December, 1823, 3rd Quarter.

offered him two boxes of ancient glass which was said to have been removed from the top of the great west window of the chapel, for the windows of his new church. On 25 May 1850 H. N. Middleton, of Bradford Peverell, visited New College to see this glass. It has been said that it was identical with the glass sent to Winchester.[1] If so, it must have been returned to New College sometime between 1845 and 1850. The glass was placed in the hands of 'an eminent glass painter', Nockalls J. Cottingham. He reported that there were 124 feet of ancient glass: 'there was little figure work amongst it, but a large quantity of rich plain colour and diaper work which he thought could be worked into draperies of figures, &c. Amongst it was the sacred monogram I.H.S., each letter on a separate piece of glass and surmounted by a crown—a very unusual arrangement. There was also much beautiful canopy work.'[2] Middleton said that Cottingham incorporated some of this glass in the present glazing of the east window: 'the drapery of our Lord in the vesica piscis, and of the angels and saints, and the white border, are ancient, but the design and the remainder of the glass is modern.'[3] It has also been said that other parts of the window are ancient, that 'some of the glass has been retouched', and that Cottingham 'proposed to use the 14th century glass, including some of the canopy work, in a second window, but this suggestion was not carried out, and, with the exception of some fragments still in Mr. Middleton's possession, the remainder of the glass was lost'.[2] It is difficult to believe that Cottingham did, in fact, use more than a very few pieces of ancient glass in his east window.

On the occasion of the visit of the Archaeological Institute to Oxford in 1852 Winston read a very able paper 'On the Painted Glass in New College Chapel and Hall, Oxford'.[4] In this paper he shows that the glass in the east window of each aisle of the ante-chapel had been seriously disarranged. He knew nothing of Taylor's activities in 1775–7, but it was clearly Taylor's doing.

In 1847 John Bradfield, of 50 Broad Street, Oxford, received £137. 7s. 4d. 'for repairing cleaning and refixing etc. the South Windows in the Chapel'. In 1848 a storm damaged the glass in

<hr />

[1] W. M. Barnes, 'A Brief Historical & Descriptive Sketch of the Churches in the Rural Deanery of Dorchester', *Proceedings of the Dorset Nat. Hist. & Antiq. Field Club*, xii. 68, fn. 1.

[2] Ibid. 69.

[3] *Proceedings of the Dorset Nat. Hist. & Antiq. Field Club*, xvi, p. xxix.

[4] Subsequently printed in *Archaeol. Journ.* ix. 29–59, 120, and in *Memoirs illustrative of the Art of Glass-painting*, 130–59.

the great west window. The stonework which had been removed for the display of the Reynolds–Jervais 'Nativity' was thereafter replaced by Messrs. Knowles and Son, of Holywell, Oxford, and Bradfield received £110 for his part in the work of restoration.[1]

In 1865, during Sir Gilbert Scott's restoration of the hall, the heraldic glass was removed from its windows to the window over the hall stairway, being replaced by stained glass, including shields of arms.

John Eastwick, Fellow 1808–62, died on 10 August 1862. He 'by his will left all that was due to him on account of his Fellowship (the proceeds of which he had allowed to accumulate in the Bursar's hands from year to year) to the use of the College'.[2] On 11 March 1863, 'at a General Meeting it was agreed that Mr. Eastwick's Legacy (amounting as it subsequently appeared to £689–6–1) should be applied to glazing the Hall with stained Glass'. On 2 February 1865, 'it was agreed . . . that it was not expedient to incur the expense of introducing figures into the windows; and that Messrs. Clayton & Bell be requested to furnish designs for the glass, treated heraldically only'.[3] Messrs. Clayton and Bell received £532 for the work.

During the time (1860–1903) that J. E. Sewell was Warden, it was decided that Peckitt's figures of Adam and Eve were insufficiently clothed, so Adam was given a leopard's skin and Eve a purple garment. Their fig-leaves have not been entirely hidden.

Between 1895 and 1900 Messrs. James Powell and Sons took out and releaded all the medieval glass in the ante-chapel. The glass in the east window of each aisle was rearranged according to Winston's reconstruction. They also repaired the glass in the great west window and plated it on both sides.

In 1932 Mr. Harry Grylls releaded the easternmost window on the north side of the choir. Some figures were removed from the tracery lights and copies, painted by Mr. Grylls, were substituted for them. In 1933 he releaded the tracery lights of the adjoining window.

In 1933–5 the rest of the choir windows were repaired by Misses C. C. Townsend and J. Howson.

In 1937 the glass in the great west window was cleaned and

---

[1] Long Books for 1847–8; Order Book of the Warden and Thirteen, March 1848; *New College Record*, 1937–8, 5.
[2] J. E. Sewell, Registrum Custodum, Sociorum, et Scholarium, Collegii Novi.
[3] Pages from a College minute book.

repaired by Messrs. R. Thomas and Son of Oxford with the help of the College workmen.

In 1939 the glass in the ante-chapel was removed by Messrs. R. Thomas and Son and placed in safe storage. The work of replacement was begun in December 1945. The medieval glass was replaced by Miss J. Howson. The opportunity was taken to plate some faces and other fragile glass and to remove pieces of glass which was of a later date than the original glazing. The positions of some of the figures, especially of the prophets, were altered and there was also some alteration of the names of saints and of parts of the votive inscriptions. The glass in the great west window was plated and replaced by the Cotswold Casement Company, Moreton-in-the-Marsh. The whole work was completed in 1948.

II

THREE EARLIER DESCRIPTIONS
OF THE GLASS

NOTICE must be taken of three earlier descriptions of the glass.
In the sixteenth century Richard Lee recorded shields of arms in the hall, and,

'In the Lyberary.
The See of Bath and Wells
    Over it written, Tho. Bekynton, bishop of bathe.

Sa. on an inescutcheon between three sugar-loaves Arg. a doctor's cap Sa.
    Over it written, Hugh Shuger, docter.'[1]

These shields and inscriptions disappeared within the next hundred years, for Anthony Wood speaks of them as 'arms sometime in the windows of the Law Library'.[2]

Thomas Beckington became a Fellow of New College in 1408 and was Bishop of Bath and Wells 1443–65. Beckington had an affectionate regard for Winchester College and New College and was a friend of Thomas Chaundler, a native of Wells, Warden of Winchester (1450) and of New College (1453).[3] He presented many books, including works on the law, to the College.

Hugh Sugar (*al.* Norris) became a Fellow of New College in 1435 and canon and Treasurer of Wells Cathedral in 1460. He died in 1489. His chantry chapel on the south side of the nave of Wells cathedral is well known. It has been noted that 'extruxit Bibliothecam librorum Judicorum [*sic*]'.[4] He gave much plate and some books to the College. The following entry is interesting in this connexion:

'Et solutum servienti maioris domus yng' pro vectura librorum Collegio datorum per doctorem Sugar, vi s. viii d.

Et solutum pro Expensis magistri Ashekum et famuli secum equitanti Welliam pro adquirendis bonis datis collegio ex dono doctoris Sugar. x s.'[5]

---

[1] *Visitation of the County of Oxford*, &c. 95.

[2] *The History and Antiquities of the Colleges and Halls in the University of Oxford*, ed. J. Gutch, Oxford, 1786, 198.

[3] *Official Correspondence of Thomas Bekynton*, ed. G. Williams, Rolls Series, 1872, i. pp. xlviii–liv, 264–76; ii. 311–26.

[4] Registrum Custodum, Sociorum, et Scholarium, Collegii Novi.

[5] AR. 4–5 Henry VII.

Anthony Wood is more informative than Richard Lee about the heraldic glass in the hall.[1] A great deal of the glass is preserved in the window over the stairway to the hall and is described fully below.[2] Wood's description of the glass may be summarized:

Windows on the northern side of the hall, reading from the east,

I. 1. St. George. 2. The Royal Arms. 3. The See of Canterbury. 4. The See of Canterbury impaling Warham.

The third shield has gone.

II. 1. The Royal Arms. 2. Wykeham or New College.

A fourteenth-century shield showing the Royal Arms survives: it could have come from this window or from the previous window.

III. 1. Wykeham or New College. 2. The See of Winchester.

The second shield has gone. A shield with the arms of Wykeham or New College could have come from this window or from the previous window.

IV. 1. St. George. 2. See of Winchester. 3. Symeon. 4. Sugar. 5. See of Winchester (a variant).

A shield showing the arms of St. George, which has survived, could have come from this window or from the first window. Shields 2, 3, and 4 are lost. Wood says of shields 3, 4, 5, 'here also have been these Arms, but long since defaced': nevertheless, shield 5 survives. Gutch adds this note, 'This fourth window has been walled up for some years; the Arms in the several windows have been transposed: and in the third window on the north side is placed the Coat of Oliver Cromwell's Commonwealth, inverted'. The window was opened again in 1805.

Geoffrey Symeon became a Fellow of New College in 1468. He held important ecclesiastical preferments, culminating in the deanery of Lincoln. He died in 1508. He gave wine to the College in 1484–5 and bequeathed £66. 13s. 4d. 'ad usum ornamenti Ecclesiae'. The money was spent in buying from William Weston a set of rich vestments for use on the principal Feasts.[3]

Southern side of the hall.

I. 1. Cranley or the Abbey of St. Edmundsbury. 2. Edward the Confessor. 3. Prince Edward, son of Henry VIII. 4. Henry VIII.

The second shield has gone.

II. 1. Sherburne. 2. Gardiner. 3. . . . . 4. Knight. 5. Longland.

Wood ascribes the fifth shield to John Longland, 1473–1547,

---

[1] *History and Antiquities of the Colleges and Halls in the University of Oxford*, 194–5.
[2] See pp. 93–4.   [3] AR. 1–2 Henry VIII.

F

Bishop of Lincoln 1521–47.[1] Edward Longland, of Kinlott, Salop, was elected a Fellow of New College in 1538. In 1539 an Edward Longland was collated to the prebendal stall of South Scarle in Lincoln cathedral. He was rector of Tingewick, a New College living, and Archdeacon of Buckingham. He died before 25 August 1549.

'In another window', 1. Symeon. 2. Sugar.

Wood makes no attempt to describe the glass in the chapel windows. He simply says, 'In several windows of the Chapel is this Inscription: Orate pro Willo de Wykeham Episcopo Wynton Fundatore istius Collegii.' Gutch added a short note on the glass which begins:

'The painted Windows are of four sorts: first, the Windows of the Ante-Chapel, (the great one excepted) which are generally supposed to be as old as the Chapel itself, and contains the Figures of Patriarchs, Prophets, Saints, Martyrs, &c. Secondly, the Windows on the south side of the Chapel, which were originally Flemish; done, as it is reported, from designs given by some Scholars of Rubens; and were purchased by the Society of Will. Price, who repaired them in 1740.'[2]

Gutch's statement has been repeated in many subsequent descriptions of the glass. It is manifestly incorrect. Such glass as is not medieval is certainly of Price's painting. Three strands may have been used in the weaving of the legend. First, the incorporation of the medieval glass in Price's panels, which, as the inscription shows, he regarded as 'repairs'.[3] Second, some memory of van Linge's work on the windows in 1634–5. Third, Price may have come by some Flemish drawings or cartoons for stained glass. Some of the figures of the female saints, such as those in the lower part of the westernmost windows, are better drawn than the other figures and may have been based on some such cartoons.

---

[1] For this formidable and forbidding man see *Dictionary of National Biography*, xxxiv. 120–1.

[2] *History and Antiquities of the Colleges and Halls in the University of Oxford*, 199, fn. 103.

[3] See above, p. 19.

III

DESCRIPTION OF THE GLASS

1. THE CHAPEL

WYKEHAM's scheme of glazing is plain enough in its general outline. The great west window was filled with a 'Tree of Jesse' and, in the tracery lights, a 'Doom'. The two other windows in the west wall, the two windows in the north wall of the north transept, and the window in the south wall of the south transept contained what may be called two 'approaches to Christ'. In the upper range of lights were twenty prophets having scrolls inscribed with messianic texts. In the lower range of lights were twenty personages, beginning with Adam and Eve, representing the Old Dispensation.

The New Dispensation is introduced in the two eastern windows of the ante-chapel. The twelve lower lights have the crucifix with the attendant figures of the Blessed Virgin Mary and St. John Evangelist four times repeated. Although the crucifixes have been largely destroyed, the significance of the repetition is clear: the redemptive power of Christ's Sacrifice was shown not only by the crucified Figures, but also by the angels issuing from clouds and receiving into chalices the Blood from the Wounds. When the four altars were in place below these roods, their meaning must have been unmistakable. In the twelve upper lights were the twelve Apostles, who were so carefully named by Wykeham in his directions for the observance of their festivals in the chapel.[1]

The eighty main lights of the choir windows contained single figures of saints beneath canopies.

Nearly all the tracery lights of the chapel were filled with representations of the Nine Orders of Angels. The exceptions are these: in the tracery lights of the great west window, a 'Doom': in the upper tracery lights of the north-east window of the ante-chapel, William of Wykeham kneeling before the Holy Trinity: in the upper tracery lights of the south-east window of the ante-chapel, the Coronation of the Blessed Virgin Mary: in the easternmost window on the north side of the choir, the Wise Virgins.

By the time that Wykeham chose the 'Tree of Jesse' for the

---

[1] *Liber Statutorum Collegii Beatae Mariae Wyntoniensis in Oxonia*, 108.

west window of New College chapel and the east window of Winchester College chapel, it had become a very popular subject in English medieval art.[1] Its symbolism appealed to the medieval mind. It was highly decorative. It could be easily expanded or contracted according to the space that had to be filled. It was used to decorate domestic wall-hangings and ecclesiastical vestments.[2] It was painted in manuscripts and on the walls of churches. Later on, it was carved on a screen and a bench-end. Nowhere was it more frequently seen than in the windows of churches. There are fifteen or more examples of fourteenth-century date, and doubtless some of those of which only written records remain belong to the same period.

It is not unlikely that the representation of prophets with scrolls bearing messianic texts had some connexion with the drama of the medieval Church. At Christmas-time there were dramatic performances in which prophets appeared and uttered prophecies concerning Christ's advent. These plays are said to have been based on a sermon entitled 'Contra Iudaeos, Paganos, et Arianos Sermo de Symbolo'. This sermon, written in the fourth or the fifth century, was attributed to St. Augustine throughout the Middle Ages, but this attribution is now discredited. At first the number of prophets was few, but in a fourteenth-century Rouen play twenty-eight persons appeared, including all the major and minor prophets of the Bible.[3]

A further development in the artistic representation of the prophets was to limit their number to twelve and to pair them off with the twelve Apostles.[4] They were given texts which tallied, as far as possible, with the sentences of the Apostles' Creed, which were written upon scrolls borne by the Apostles. This combination of the prophets and Apostles is sometimes found in the art of fourteenth-century England, but became much more popular in the following century.

Amos and Isaiah almost always have the texts (Amos ix. 6) *Qui aedificat in caelo ascensionem suam* and (Isaiah vii. 14) *Ecce*

---

[1] The origins of the subject are fully examined by A. Watson in *The Early Iconography of the Tree of Jesse*, Oxford, 1934.

[2] Wykeham's will has, 'Item lego Ecclesiae meae Winton. vestimentum novum de blodio panno, virgato & operato cum leonibus de auro, cum viginti capis de eodem panno aurifrigiatis cum historia de Jesse'. Lowth, *The Life of William of Wykeham, Bishop of Winchester*, appendix xvii, p. xxxviii.

[3] See 'The Procession of Prophets' in K. Young's *The Drama of the Medieval Church*, Oxford, 1933, ii. 125–71: Watson, *The Early Iconography of the Tree of Jesse*, 9–36, 148–61.

[4] The association of the prophets and Apostles in art is found as early as the fifth century.

virgo concipiet et pariet filium. Hosea almost always has (Hosea xiii. 14) *O mors ero mors tua morsus tuus ero inferne,* but on the screen at Kenton, Devon, it is combined with words from Hosea vi. 2. With the single exception of glass in King's College chapel, Cambridge, David has (Psalm ii. 7) *Dominus dixit ad me: Filius meus es tu; ego hodie genui te.* Otherwise the texts given to the prophets vary considerably. Sometimes a prophet is given a text from the writings of another prophet, a practice too systematic to be explained by the supposition that they have been wrongly named. For instance, in the fourteenth-century Queen Mary's Psalter, on the fifteenth-century screen at Thornham, Norfolk, and in the Fairford glass Micah has a text from Zephaniah iii. 9 and Zephaniah has, as so often, a text from Micah iii. 5. Similarly, Daniel several times has a text from Ezekiel xxxvii. 12 and Ezekiel, when he does not have that text, generally has a text from Daniel xii. 2.

Five more prophets are needed to complete the series of prophets in the ante-chapel windows. One of these may have been Elijah, or Samuel, of whom indications perhaps remain.[1] Haggai, Obadiah, and Zechariah are obvious omissions. Eight more patriarchs are needed. To name them would be mere guesswork, but it should be remembered that the remaining figures may have been telescoped and that such figures as Melchisedech and Lot may have been represented in the early part of the series.

Wykeham probably chose his saints from a calendar or litany of the Sarum Use. There is, however, another possibility. The 'Liber Vitae' of New Minster, otherwise Hyde abbey, in Winchester contains a list of 'saints who happily rule in the Kingdom of Heaven', written about 1016. The list begins with Adam and includes more than fifty Old Testament patriarchs and prophets; it passes on to St. John Baptist and the Apostles, and thence to the early popes. Unfortunately it is incomplete and it is not known what later saints were included.[2] It is possible that Wykeham had something of the kind before him when he was choosing his saints. His choice may also have been influenced by the relics which reposed at Winchester. There is no record of the relics possessed by the cathedral church, but Hyde abbey had a great number, and it was not difficult to divide a relic.[3] Perhaps

---

[1] See below, p. 72.
[2] *Liber Vitae: Register and Martyrology of New Minster and Hyde Abbey, Winchester,* ed. W. de G. Birch, Hampshire Record Soc., 1892, 153–4.
[3] Ibid. lxiv–vi, 147–53, 159–63.

it is not without significance that Hyde abbey had relics of Abundius, Anastasia, Columbanus, the martyrs John and Paul, and that these very unusual saints were probably all represented in the New College windows.[1]

Wykeham evidently intended that his scholars should contemplate the saints of all the ages of the Christian era. He laid emphasis on the early ecclesiastical saints and devised a full display of English saints. It is notable that in Winchester College chapel, where the space at his disposal was very much less, he omitted all the female saints except the Blessed Virgin Mary, St. Anne, and St. Mary Magdalene. It is unfortunate that there is no full list of the saints represented or description of the order in which they were placed. Some saints, of whom no trace now remains, would certainly have been represented. Birinus, Swithun, Ethelwold, and Wulstan would have been included among the male saints and probably Frideswide among the female saints. Other saints who are shown in Winchester College chapel and might be expected to be represented at New College are Edward the Confessor, Giles, Leonard, Martin, and Nicholas. Wykeham specifically names Martin and Nicholas, together with Michael, Luke, and Thomas Becket, as saints whose festivals must be observed in the chapel.[2] If the position of the figures as shown in Purnell's plan indicates the original order, in the three westerly windows on the south side of the choir male saints occupied the upper lights and female saints the lower lights. It might be expected that virgin saints occupied the main lights below the Wise Virgins in the easternmost window on the northern side.

The organized hierarchy of angels is said to have its origin in Jewish apocryphal literature. The Nine Orders, best known in the later Middle Ages through the *Golden Legend*, are first found in a Greek treatise, 'On the Celestial Hierarchy', which was attributed to Dionysius the Areopagite but was written in the fifth or sixth century. There were three 'hierarchies': first, Seraphim, Cherubim, Thrones; second, Dominations, Virtues, Powers; third, Principalities, Archangels, Angels. The hierarchies were devised by putting together St. Paul's list of supernatural beings (Ephesians i. 21: Colossians i. 16), the cherubim (Ezekiel x), the seraphim (Isaiah vi. 2), the archangels (1

---

[1] St. Columbanus was also remembered in the litany at Hyde abbey, see *The Monastic Breviary of Hyde Abbey, Winchester*, v, ed. J. B. L. Tolhurst, Henry Bradshaw Society Publications, lxxi, f. G.66 v.

[2] *Liber Statutorum Collegii Beatae Mariae Wyntoniensis in Oxonia*, 108.

Thessalonians iv. 16: Jude 9, &c.), and the angels so often mentioned in the Bible.[1]

The parable of the Wise and the Foolish Virgins was a favourite subject for artists in the thirteenth century. The figures were associated with the Last Judgement because they symbolized the elect and the lost.[2] A fine example (*c.* 1270–80) is carved on the tympanum over the south doorway of the 'Angel Choir' in Lincoln cathedral.[3] The parable is represented in a window in Melbury Bubb church, Dorset: the glass was probably given by Walter Bokeler, who was instituted to the benefice in 1466.

NORTH AISLE. WEST WINDOW

TRACERIES. The angels are feathered to their elbows and thighs and have four wings. They wear diadems, surmounted by crosses, and knotted scarves round their necks and waists. Their hands are raised in adoration. Thrones are depicted behind their legs. In the two upper lights the left-hand angel stands against a blue background and the right-hand angel against a red background. They stand upon murrey pedestals and are named *Troni*. The angels in the four lower lights are set against blue and red backgrounds and stand upon green mounds.

MAIN LIGHTS. UPPER TIER

1. JEREMIAH. The backgrounds of the canopy, figure, and pedestal upon which the prophet stands are blue and, behind the figure, are powdered with the letter *I*. Jeremiah wears a purple robe, green mantle, red headgear, and murrey shoes. He stands upon a black and white chequered pavement. His scroll bears *Patrē vocabis me dicit dn̄s* (part of Jeremiah iii. 19–20, *Patrem vocabis me . . . dicit dominus*, 'Thou shalt call me . . . father . . . saith the Lord'). Beneath, *Ieremias · ppha·*.

The text usually given to Jeremiah is a combination of Jeremiah iii. 19 and xxxii. 17.

2. ISAIAH. The backgrounds of the upper part of the canopy and of the figure are red, the background of the figure being

---

[1] For the complicated iconography of the Nine Orders of Angels see P. B. Chatwin, 'The Decoration of the Beauchamp Chapel, Warwick, with special reference to the Sculptures', *Archaeologia*, lxxvii. 316–7; G. McN. Rushforth, *Medieval Christian Imagery*, Oxford, 1936, 204–16; C. Woodforde, *The Norwich School of Glass-painting in the Fifteenth Century*, Oxford, 1950.

[2] Émile Mâle, *Religious Art in France: XII Century*, trans. D. Nussey, London, 1913, 197–9, gives the full symbolism of the parable.

[3] A. Gardner, *A Handbook of English Medieval Sculpture*, Cambridge, 1935, 166–9, figs. 200–1.

powdered with the letter *Y*. The backgrounds of the lower part of the canopy and of the pedestal are blue. Isaiah wears a brown robe, blue mantle, green headgear, and murrey shoes. He stands upon a black and white chequered pavement. His scroll bears *ec(ce virg)o concipiet & pariet filium* (Isaiah vii. 14, 'Behold, a virgin shall conceive, and bear a son'). Beneath, *Ysaias · ppta*.

3. A PATRIARCH OR PROPHET. The backgrounds of the canopy and of the figure are blue, the background of the figure being powdered with the letter *S*. The background of the pedestal is murrey. The man wears a white robe, purple mantle, and green headgear. The scroll and name are made up of scraps of lettering, *Ew, A, M, S · Ig, c̄a · C, nast, u'*. and *S, a, c̄a, ri, c̄s, nta*.

If the background originally belonged to this figure and if the figure was of a prophet, it may represent Samuel. There is a fourteenth-century stained-glass figure of Samuel in Bale church, Norfolk; he has a text from 1 Samuel xiv. 13.

Pieces of the name *Maria Salome*, taken from a light in the east window of the north aisle, were used to make up the scroll and the name. Other pieces suggest *(Sc)s · Ig(natius ·), (S)c̄a · C(ristina ·)* or *(S)ca · C(ecilia), (Scā) · Anast(asia)*, St. Ignatius, St. Cristina, and St. Cecilia were represented on the south side of the choir. St. Anastasia is among the saints in fifteenth-century glass in the chapel of All Souls College.

4. HOSEA. The backgrounds of the canopy and figure are red, the background of the figure being powdered with the letter *H*. The background of the pedestal is purple. Hosea wears a white robe, made up with murrey glass, purple mantle, green headgear and shoes. His scroll bears *O · mors · ero · (mo)rs · tua · morsus · tuus · ero · inferne* (Hosea xiii. 14, 'O death, I will be thy plagues; O grave, I will be thy destruction'). Beneath, *Osee · ppheta ·*.

It is unlikely that the background originally belonged to this figure; it should be powdered with the letter *O*. If it stood behind the figure of a prophet, that prophet may have been Elijah. His figure from the 'Tree of Jesse' window is named *Helias · pp*.

LOWER TIER

1. ADAM. The backgrounds of the canopy and pedestal are blue. The red background of the figure is powdered with the letter *A*. Adam wears a long, white robe, with an edging of yellow fur, girded with a narrow, black and white belt. He stands bare-footed on green ground and holds a spade stained yellow and painted to represent grained wood; the cutting edge of the

spade is shod with metal, which is represented in white glass. Beneath, *Adā · pm' · pa(ter)*, (*Adam primus pater*).

2. EVE. The backgrounds of the canopy and pedestal are red. A sun is placed on either side of the pedestal. The blue background of the figure is powdered with the letter *E*. Eve wears a white robe, girded with a narrow, yellow girdle, and a white veil. She spins. Beneath, *Eua : M̄r · ōiū · uiūeciū* (*Eva Mater omnium viventium*). In the last word, *uiūe* is inverted and *ciū* appears to be modern.

3. SETH. The backgrounds of the canopy and pedestal are blue. The red background of the figure is powdered with the letter *S*. Seth wears a purple robe and headgear, green mantle, and blue shoes. Beneath, *Seth · filius · ade'*.

4. ENOCH. The backgrounds of the canopy and pedestal are red. The blue background of the figure is powdered with the letter *E*. Enoch wears a white robe, with yellow, ornamental edging, murrey mantle and headgear, and purple shoes. He stands on a black and white chequered pavement and holds (the hand is now missing) a scroll inscribed *uixit cū deo*. Beneath, *Enoch translat'·*.

Across the pedestals in the lower part of the window is this inscription, *Orate · p · Willm̄o · de · Wykeham̄ · episcopo · Wynton' · fūdator' · istius · collegii*.

NORTH AISLE. WEST WINDOW IN NORTH WALL

TRACERIES. The angels have two wings and wear armour. Each angel has his inner hand raised with palm outwards and holds in his outer hand a spear, to which is attached a pennon bearing a cross. In the two upper lights, the left-hand angel is set against a blue background and the right-hand angel against a red background. They stand upon murrey pedestals. Beneath, *Prin · ci · pa · tus ·*. The four lower figures are set against alternating blue and red backgrounds. They stand upon alternating green and yellow pedestals, the backgrounds of which alternate with those behind the figures.

MAIN LIGHTS. UPPER TIER

1. AMOS. The background of the canopy is blue. The red background of the figure is powdered with the letter *A*. The background of the pedestal is purple. Amos wears a white robe, blue mantle, yellow headgear, murrey hose, and green shoes. His scroll bears *qui · (aed)ificat · in · celo · assencōnē · suā* (Amos ix. 6,

Qui aedificat in caelo ascensionem suam, 'It is he that buildeth his stories in heaven'). Beneath, *Amos · ppheta ·*.

2. JOEL. The backgrounds of the canopy and pedestal are red. The blue background of the figure is powdered with the letter *I*. Joel wears a white robe, red mantle, yellow headgear and shoes, and murrey hose. His scroll bears *In valle iosaphat indicavit o͞es g͞etes* (Joel iii. 12, *Consurgant, et ascendant gentes in vallem Josaphat; quia ibi sedebo ut judicem omnes gentes in circuitu,* 'Let the heathen be wakened, and come up to the valley of Jehoshaphat; for there will I sit to judge all the heathen round about'). Beneath, *Iohel · ppheta ·*.

This text is given to Joel in the Fairford glass and on the screen at Kenton, Devon. The text usually given to him is Joel ii. 28.

3. MICAH. The backgrounds of the canopy and figure are blue, the background of the figure being powdered with the letter *M*. The background of the pedestal is red. Micah wears a white robe, green mantle, purple headgear, and murrey shoes. His scroll bears *De · (Si)on · exibit · lex · et · uerbū · d · · ·* (based on Micah iv. 2, *de Sion egredietur lex, et verbum Domini de Jerusalem,* 'for the law shall go forth of Zion, and the word of the Lord from Jerusalem'). Beneath, *Micheas · pphā*.

Micah generally has a text from Micah vii. 19, but, as has already been said, he is sometimes given a text from Zephaniah iii. 9.

4. ZEPHANIAH. The backgrounds of the canopy and figure are red, the background of the figure being powdered with the letter *S*. The background of the pedestal is purple. Zephaniah wears a white robe, purple mantle, blue headgear, and green shoes. His scroll bears *Hec · est · ciuitas · g͞lriosa · quia · dicit · ego · sum* (Zephaniah ii. 15, *Haec est civitas gloriosa habitans in confidentia quae dicebat: Ego sum, et extra me non est alia amplius,* 'This is the rejoicing city that dwelt carelessly, that said in her heart, I am, and there is none beside me'). Beneath, *Sophonias · ppha ·*.

On the screen at Kenton this text is combined with Revelation xxi. 2. In fifteenth-century stained glass at Stratford St. Mary, Suffolk, the text is from Zephaniah iii. 9. Elsewhere Zephaniah is given the text from Malachi iii. 5.

LOWER TIER

1. METHUSELAH. The backgrounds of the canopy and pedestal are blue. The red background of the figure is powdered with the letter *M*. Methuselah wears a white robe with yellow edging,

green mantle, blue headgear, and purple shoes. He stands on a black and white chequered pavement. He holds a scroll, the lettering on which reads *Legem: n: roM.* Beneath, *Matusale · filīs · Enoch ·.*

2. NOAH. The backgrounds of the canopy and pedestal are red. A sun is placed on either side of the pedestal. The blue background of the figure is powdered with the letter *N*. Noah wears a white robe, purple mantle and headgear, and brown shoes. In his right hand he holds an oar, which has a yellow shaft and murrey blade. He stands on a black and yellow chequered pavement. Beneath, *Noe q̄ᶦ archā fabᶦca.*

3. ABRAHAM. The background of the canopy is murrey. The red background of the figure is powdered with the letter *A*. The background of the pedestal is blue. Abraham wears a white robe, purple mantle, blue cap, and pink shoes. He holds a brown book in his right hand and stands on a green mound. Beneath, *Abrahā p̄riarcha.*

4. ISAAC. The backgrounds of the canopy and pedestal are red. A sun is placed on each side of the pedestal. The blue background of the figure is powdered with the letter *I*. He wears a white robe, murrey mantle, and purple hat and shoes. He stands upon a black and white chequered pavement. His face is very incomplete. Beneath, *Isaac · patriarcha.*

Across the pedestals in the lower part of the window, *Orate · p · Willm̄o · de · Wykehm̄ · epo · Wynton · fundator' · istius (·) colleg(ii ·).*

NORTH AISLE. EAST WINDOW IN NORTH WALL

TRACERIES. The angels are represented as royal personages. They have two wings each and wear white tunics, with vair tippets, golden collars, and golden trefoiled crowns. They carry each a white sword and yellow sceptre. In the two upper lights, the left-hand angel is set against a blue background and the right-hand angel is set against a red background. They stand upon murrey pedestals. Beneath, *Dña · cio · nes.* The four lower figures are set against alternating blue and red backgrounds. They stand upon alternating green and yellow pedestals, the backgrounds of which alternate with those behind the figures.

MAIN LIGHTS. UPPER TIER

1. DANIEL. The backgrounds of the canopy and pedestal are red. The blue background of the figure is powdered with the letter *D*. Daniel wears a white robe, red mantle, green headgear and shoes. His scroll bears *Post ebdomadas septuaginta duas occit'*

(Daniel ix. 26, *Et post hebdomadas sexaginta duas occidetur Christus,*
'And after three score and two weeks shall Messiah be cut off').
Beneath, *Daniel · ppheta ·.*

2. EZEKIEL. The background of the canopy is blue. The background of the pedestal is murrey; two suns are placed on each
side of the pedestal. The upper part of the figure is set on a background which is powdered with the letter *E.* Ezekiel wears a
white robe, green mantle, and purple headgear. His scroll bears
Visitabo oues meas & liberabo ea(s) (Ezekiel xxxiv. 12, 'I will seek
out my sheep, and will deliver them'). The lower part of the
figure is lost and its place is taken by the lower part of another
figure, which is set upon a blue background powdered with the
letter *M.* This figure wears a red robe, white mantle, and green
shoes. Beneath, the name is fragmentary, *E, ci, a, s, ppheta.*

3. OBADIAH. The background of the canopy is murrey. The
blue background of the figure is powdered with the letter *A.*
The background of the pedestal is red. Obadiah wears a white
robe, yellow mantle, and purple shoes. His head is lost and has
been replaced by the head of a youthful male saint. His scroll
bears *Et · regnm · erit · dnm · dñi · amen* (Obadiah 21, *Et erit Domino
regnum,* 'And the kingdom shall be the Lord's'). Beneath, *Abdias·
pphā ·.*

4. HABAKKUK. The backgrounds of the canopy and figure are
blue, the background of the figure being powdered with the
letter *A.* The background of the pedestal is red. Habakkuk wears
a white robe, murrey mantle, purple headgear and shoes. His
scroll bears *Dñe audiui auditionē tuā & timui* (Habakkuk iii. 2,
Domine, audivi auditionem tuam, et timui, 'O Lord, I have heard thy
speech, and was afraid'). Beneath, *Abacuch · pphā·.*

In the fourteenth-century 'Tree of Jesse' painted on the ceiling
of the Lady aisle in St. Helen's church, Abingdon, Habakkuk
has a text from Habakkuk ii. 3. In sixteenth-century glass at
Withcote, near Oakham, his text is from Habakkuk iii. 18.

LOWER TIER

1. JACOB. The backgrounds of the canopy and pedestal are
blue. The red background of the figure is powdered with the
letter *I.* Jacob wears a white robe, green mantle, purple headgear, and blue shoes. He holds a white book in his left hand.
Beneath, *Iacob · ppriar.*

2. JUDAH. The background of the canopy is blue. The backgrounds of the figure and pedestal are red, the background of
the figure being powdered with the letter *I.* A sun is placed on

each side of the base. Judah wears a white robe, diapered with the crowned letter *I*, and green mantle. He wears a golden fillet on his head and holds a blue sceptre. He stands on a black and white chequered pavement. Beneath, *Iudas Macobeus*.

This figure undoubtedly represents Judah (Genesis xlix. 10, 'The sceptre shall not depart from Judah'). The chance conjunction of his name with the letters *Ma* led Winston to think that Judas Maccabeus was here represented, and Messrs. Powell supplied the rest of his name.[1] *Ma* could be the beginning of the name *Manasseh*.

3. Moses. The backgrounds of the canopy and pedestal are blue. The red background of the figure is powdered with the letter *M*. Moses wears a white robe, purple mantle, and green shoes. Brown horns spring from his head. He holds green tables of the Law in his right hand. They are inscribed thus

RV	*ID*
B̄V̄	*ER*
ŌC̄	*AT*
MV	*MO*

Beneath, *Moyses · dux · Pli · dei ·*.

Horns or, less often, rays of light are the distinguishing mark of Moses. The Hebrew verb for 'shone' in 'the skin of his face shone' (Exodus xxxiv. 30) is also the root of the noun meaning 'horn'; the Vulgate rendering, *facies cornuta*, was literally interpreted by artists as far back as the eleventh century.

4. Nahum and Aaron. The background of the canopy and base is red. A sun is placed on each side of the base. The upper part of a figure of Nahum is set against a red background, which is powdered with the letter *N*. Nahum wears a white robe and blue mantle. His scroll bears *Ecce sup(er) montes pedes ewāgelisa(n)tis et annūciātis (pacem)* (Nahum i. 15, *Ecce super montes pedes evangelizantis, et annuntiantis pacem*, 'Behold upon the mountains the feet of him that bringeth good tidings, that publisheth peace'). Nahum has this text in the fourteenth-century 'Tree of Jesse' in the east window of Morpeth church, Northumberland. The lower part of the figure is lost and its place is taken by the lower part of a figure of Aaron, which is set against a blue background, powdered with the letter *A*. Aaron wears white and murrey vestments and purple shoes. He stands on a black and white chequered pavement. Beneath, *Aar̄o · sūm' · sac'rdos ·*.

[1] Winston, 'The Painted Glass in New College Chapel and Hall, Oxford', *Memoirs illustrative of the Art of Glass-painting*, 135.

Across the pedestals in the lower part of the window, *Orate ·
p · Willm̄o(·) de · Wykehm̄ · epo · Wyntoñ · fūdator' · istius · collegii ·*.

NORTH AISLE. EAST WINDOW

TRACERIES. The two upper lights contain a representation of
William of Wykeham kneeling before Christ enthroned and showing His Wounds. Both figures, Wykeham on the right and Christ
enthroned on the left, are placed beneath canopies and against
blue backgrounds. The eight main tracery lights below contain
angels which alternately hold trumpets and sceptres. These
angels are feathered and have six wings. They wear diadems on
their heads and knotted scarves round their necks and waists.
The 'Archangels' in the third window from the east on the
north side of the choir hold trumpets.

MAIN LIGHTS. UPPER TIER

1. ST. PETER. He wears a blue robe and white mantle, and has
a purple nimbus. He holds two yellow keys and a murrey book.
Beneath, *Sc̄s · Petru'*.

2. ST. ANDREW. He wears a red robe and white mantle, and
has a murrey nimbus. His face is of fifteenth-century or later
glass. There is a suggestion of a saltire cross, but this may be a
later insertion. Beneath, *Sc̄s · Andrea'*.

3. ST. JAMES THE GREATER. He wears a murrey robe and hat,
and a white mantle. He holds a white staff. Beneath, *Sc̄s Iacobu'*.

The colour of St. James's robe is a break in the alternating red
and blue of the other robes. If Betton and Evans's reproduction
of the Apostles in Winchester College chapel is faithful (and
there is no reason to doubt it), St. James had a robe of the same
colour there.

4. ST. JOHN. He wears a red robe and white mantle, and has a
murrey nimbus. His face is of fifteenth-century or later glass.
He holds in his right hand a yellow chalice, from which emerges
a demon with a white body and yellow wings, and in his left hand
a green palm. Beneath, *Sc̄s · Iohaēs*.

5. ST. THOMAS. He wears a blue robe and white mantle, and
has a green nimbus. His emblem (a spear) is lost. Beneath, *Sc̄s ·
Thoma'*.

6. ST. JAMES THE LESS. He wears a red robe and white mantle,
and has a murrey nimbus. He holds a falchion. Beneath, *Sc̄s · Iacob ·*.

This is one of the figures that illustrates the close affinity of
this series with the series at All Souls College and Winchester
College. The emblem almost invariably given to St. James the

Less is a fuller's club.[1] At New College, All Souls, and Winchester he holds a falchion, as he does also in earlier glass in Merton College chapel and in later glass in Melbury Bubb church, Dorset. The probable reason for this emblem is in Acts xii. 1–2, 'About that time Herod the king stretched forth his hands to vex certain of the church. And he killed James the brother of John with the sword.' Whereas the Latin Church identified James the Less, the son of Alphaeus (Mark iii. 18, &c.), with James the brother of the Lord (Galatians i. 19; Mark vi. 37) the confusion here is between James the Less and James the Greater, the son of Zebedee and brother of John.

LOWER TIER

1. The figure of the Blessed Virgin Mary is lost and the light is filled with glass from elsewhere. There is the upper part of a figure of a female saint with long yellow hair. She wears a red robe and white mantle. She holds a book in her left hand; her right hand is placed on her breast. The blue background is powdered with the letter C and one letter A.

2. Crucifix panel. There are some remains of the glass originally belonging to this light. There is part of the red background powdered with the letter X. There are also the bottom of the murrey cross standing on a green mound and clouds on either side. These clouds show that there were attendant angels holding chalices to receive the Blood from the Wounds. Amongst the glass which fills the rest of the light are the greater part of the head of a female saint, drapery, and several examples of the letter C from a background. The drapery which is diapered with the crowned letter C, and the letters from the background belong to the figure of the female saint in the west window of the south aisle, lower tier, light 2.

3. ST. JOHN EVANGELIST. The blue background is powdered with yellow roundels enclosing the letter I. St. John wears a red robe and white mantle, and has a murrey nimbus. His right hand is raised to his face in an attitude of grief; in his left hand he holds a purple book.

4. THE BLESSED VIRGIN MARY. The red background is powdered with the letter M. The Blessed Virgin wears a blue robe and a white mantle with hood drawn over her head. She has a green nimbus. Her hands are clasped in grief.

[1] 'The earliest of Church historians, Hegesippus, told a story of this James being cast down from the Temple by the Jews, and killed with a fuller's bat or club. Hence the symbol', M. R. James, *Suffolk and Norfolk*, London, 1930, 217.

5. CRUCIFIX PANEL. The remains of the crucifix are as in light 2. The upper part of the light has portions of a figure of an ecclesiastic wearing a white alb and blue crossed stole. The crowned letter *B* is several times repeated.

6. ST. JOHN EVANGELIST. The red background is powdered with the letter *I*. St. John wears a blue robe and white mantle, and has a blue nimbus. His right hand is placed on his breast: in his left hand he holds a purple book.

Across the pedestals in the lower part of the window, *Orate · p · (Will)m̄o · de · Wykehm̄ · episc(opo) · Wyntōn · fundatore · istius · collegii(·)*.

SOUTH AISLE. EAST WINDOW

TRACERIES. The two upper lights contain a representation of the Coronation of the Blessed Virgin Mary. Both figures, the Blessed Virgin on the left and the Deity on the right, sit upon green thrones, and are placed beneath canopies and against red backgrounds. The Blessed Virgin, who is crowned and nimbed, wears a purple robe and white mantle. The Deity, who has a cruciform nimbus, wears a blue robe and a white mantle with a vair tippet. He holds an orb surmounted by a cross: part of this is of modern glass. The eight lights below contain angels in pairs. Those on the left each have two wings and wear white girded albs and apparelled amices: they have chaplets on their heads. They carry closed books in their left hands and staves in their right hands. Those on the right each have six wings and are feathered. They wear ermine tippets and have diadems on their heads. Their hands are joined in prayer. These figures represent the Order 'Angels'.

MAIN LIGHTS. UPPER TIER

1. ST. PHILIP. He wears a purple robe and white mantle, and has a blue nimbus. His face is of later glass; the paint has mostly gone from it. He holds a purple decorative cross. Beneath, *Scs · Philipu'*.

The same form of short decorative cross is held by St. Philip in the All Souls and Winchester glass. Elsewhere a long cross is sometimes given to St. Philip, who was said to have been crucified at Hierapolis. More often, as on East Anglian screens and on alabasters, he holds loaves (sometimes in a basket) in reference to the Feeding of the Five Thousand (St. John vi).[1]

---

[1] On one alabaster he holds a cup or chalice. This is a surprising emblem, but the identification is made certain by the text from the Apostles Creed on his scroll: see

2. St. Bartholomew. He wears a red robe and white mantle, and has a murrey nimbus. He holds a flaying-knife. Beneath, *Sc̄s · Bartholeme̅*. The letters *eme̅* may come from elsewhere.

3. St. Matthew. He wears a blue robe and white mantle, and has a purple nimbus. He holds a falchion. Beneath, *Sc̄s · Mathe'*.

He has a falchion at All Souls. At Winchester he has no emblem. His usual emblem is a halbert, but the *Golden Legend* says that he was executed with a sword.[1]

4. St. Simon. He wears a red robe and white mantle, and has a murrey nimbus. He holds a halbert. Beneath, *Sc̄s · Simon*.

5. St. Matthias. He wears a blue robe and white mantle, and has a purple nimbus. He holds a white club. Beneath, *Sc̄s · Mathia'*.

6. St. Jude. He wears a red robe and white mantle, and has a murrey nimbus. He has no emblem. Beneath, *Sc̄s · Iudas ·*.

The emblems of SS. Simon and Matthias are confusing. The usual emblems of SS. Simon, Jude, and Matthias are a fish, a boat, and a halbert respectively, but there are exceptions. St. Simon (now named Matthias) has a halbert at All Souls and in fifteenth-century glass at Melbury Bubb, Dorset. He is also to be seen with an oar or a saw. At Winchester he has three loaves: in the great east window of Great Malvern priory church he has a falchion: on the rood-screens at Cawston and Ringland, Norfolk, he has a club. He holds a banner on a long pole in thirteenth-century glass and perhaps also in fourteenth-century glass in Canterbury cathedral.[2] St. Jude holds a club in the Winchester glass and on the screen at Aylsham, Norfolk. At All Souls and Fairford he holds loaves.[3] In the representations of the children of Mary Cleopas in fifteenth-century glass at Hesset, Suffolk, St. Simon holds a fish and St. Jude holds loaves, and on the screen at Houghton St. Giles, Norfolk, either St. Simon or St. Jude holds loaves. St. Matthias has a halbert at Winchester: at All Souls he holds a club, although Messrs. Clayton and Bell gave him the name Jude in 1870–1: at Melbury Bubb he has a falchion.

The halbert and falchion are appropriate emblems for St. Simon: the *Golden Legend* says that he and St. Jude were hewed

P. Nelson, 'Some Unpublished English Medieval Alabaster Carvings', *Archaeol. Journ.* lxxvii. 216.

[1] *Golden Legend, or Lives of the Saints as Englished by William Caxton*, ed. F. S. Ellis, Temple Classics, London, 1900, v. 153.

[2] Rackham, *The Ancient Glass of Canterbury Cathedral*, 114, 127.

[3] At All Souls Messrs. Clayton and Bell renamed him Simon in 1870–1.

G

in pieces by heathen priests.[1] The halbert was probably given to St. Matthias because he was confused with St. Matthew.

At New College the matter is complicated by the order in which these three Apostles are placed.[2] SS. Simon and Jude should stand together and in that order.[3] St. Matthias should come last. The colour scheme suggests that the naming, not the order, of the panels is wrong. If the names of St. Matthias and St. Jude were interchanged St. Jude would hold a club, as at Winchester, and Matthias would have no emblem because the artist did not want to repeat St. Matthew's falchion or St. Simon's halbert.

LOWER TIER

1. THE BLESSED VIRGIN MARY. The blue background is powdered with the letter *M*. The Blessed Virgin wears a red robe and a white mantle with hood down over her head. She has a murrey nimbus and purple shoes. Her left hand is raised to her face: in her right hand is a book.

2. CRUCIFIX PANEL. There is the lower part of a green cross on a purple mound, with clouds on either side. It is set against a red background. The upper part of the light is filled with portions of a female saint, with a white veil and purple nimbus, set against a blue background, powdered with the letter *E*. Remains of murrey and purple drapery may belong to this figure.

3. ST. JOHN EVANGELIST. The blue background is powdered with yellow roundels. St. John wears a red robe and white mantle, and has a murrey nimbus. His right hand is raised to his face in an attitude of grief; in his left hand he holds a purple book.

4. THE BLESSED VIRGIN MARY. The red background is powdered with the letter *M*. The Blessed Virgin wears a blue robe and a white mantle with hood drawn over her head. Her hands are clasped in grief.

5. CRUCIFIX PANEL. The remains of the crucifix are as in light 2. In the upper part of the light there are portions of a figure of a female saint. She has a blue nimbus and holds a murrey palm in her right hand. The red background is powdered with the letter *M*.

---

[1] *Golden Legend*, vi. 80.

[2] They were in the present order before Powell rearranged these windows.

[3] Legend says that Simon and Jude visited Persia. Their bodies were brought together in St. Peter's, Rome, in the seventh or eighth century; thereafter they were associated on 28 October in the Western calendars.

6. St. John Evangelist. The red background is powdered with the letter *I*. St. John wears a blue robe and white mantle, and has a blue nimbus. His right hand is placed on his breast: in his left hand he holds a purple book.

Across the pedestals in the lower part of the window, *Orate · p · Willo · de · Wykehm · episcopo · Wynton · fundatore · istius · collegii*.

It is clear that the four 'roods' in these two windows were painted as pairs, but the original order in which they were placed is unknown. It is also clear that the proper order of the Crucifix panels has not been preserved: the murrey crosses on green mounds would have been associated with one pair of figures of the Blessed Virgin and St. John and the green crosses on purple mounds with the other pair.

SOUTH AISLE. SOUTH WINDOW

Traceries. The angels are feathered and have four wings. They wear diadems on their heads and knotted scarves round their necks and waists. They hold open books. In the two upper lights, the left-hand angel is set against a blue background and the right-hand angel against a red background. They stand upon green pedestals. Beneath, *Cherubin*. The four lower figures are set against alternating purple and murrey backgrounds and stand upon brown pedestals.

MAIN LIGHTS. UPPER TIER

1. A bishop. The backgrounds of the canopy and pedestal are murrey. The blue background of the figure is powdered with the letter *P*. His alb and cope are white. His amice, stole, maniple, and shoes are murrey. His mitre is ornamented in yellow stain. His crosier has the crook decorated in yellow stain and the shaft of green glass. The name is lost and is made up with fragments, *Scs, na, ci, icu, is*.

2. A pope. The backgrounds of the canopy and pedestal are murrey. The blue background is powdered with the letter *D*. He wears a white alb and a white chasuble with murrey orphrey. His amice, dalmatic, and maniple are murrey. His tunicle shows as a strip of green glass below his dalmatic. He has a papal tiara on his head and brown shoes on his feet. He holds a double-crossed pastoral staff, the cross of white and yellow stained glass, and the shaft green. The face is of later glass. Beneath, *Scs · Pelagius ·*.

There was no pope named Pelagius. Perhaps the most likely saint of that name to be represented here is Pelagius, Bishop of

Laodicea, a champion of the Church against Arianism. He was present at the Council of Constantinople in 381. Hyde abbey possessed a relic of St. Pelagius.

It seems likely that the figure was originally set upon the background now in light 1. The background upon which it is now set may have been placed behind a figure of St. Dunstan.

3. St. ALPHEGE. The backgrounds of the canopy and pedestal are murrey. The blue background of the figure is powdered with the letter *A*. Alphege wears a white alb and a white chasuble with green orphrey. His amice, dalmatic, and maniple are murrey. His green tunicle shows beneath his dalmatic. His archiepiscopal cross is shown in white and yellow-stain glass: the shaft is murrey. Beneath, *Scs · Alphegeus ·*.

St. Alphege, 954–1012, was a Benedictine of Deerhurst abbey, Gloucestershire. He succeeded Aethelwold as Bishop of Winchester in 984 and became Archbishop of Canterbury in 1006. He was killed by the Danes in 1012. His body was buried in St. Paul's, but was translated by Canute to Canterbury.

4. St. GERMANUS. The backgrounds of the canopy and pedestal are blue: a rose is placed each side of the base. The red background of the figure is powdered with the letter *G*. Germanus wears a white alb and his white chasuble has an orphrey depicted in yellow stain. His amice and dalmatic are green, and his shoes are blue. The crook of his crosier is done in white glass and yellow stain: the shaft is murrey. Beneath, the name is partly lost and now reads, *Scs Ge, ma, cta, o.*

St. Germanus, c. 378–448, was a native and Bishop of Auxerre. He came to Britain in 430 and 447 to confute the Pelagian heresy. During the first visit he led the Britons to their 'Alleluia' victory against the Picts and Scots. He is depicted in fifteenth-century stained glass in the church of Wiggenhall St. Mary Magdalene, Norfolk, and his figure was once to be seen, with that of St. Bernard, in a north window of the chancel at Eccles, Norfolk.[1] It is also possible that part of his name survives in glass in Winchester cathedral.[2]

LOWER TIER

1. St. ATHANASIUS. The background of the canopy is red and of the pedestal is murrey. The blue background of the figure is powdered with the letter *A*. Athanasius wears a white alb and

---

[1] F. Blomefield, *An Essay towards a Topographical History of the County of Norfolk*, ed. 1805, i. 410.

[2] Le Couteur, *Ancient Glass in Winchester*, 50.

a white chasuble with yellow-stain orphrey. His amice and dalmatic are purple, and his shoes murrey. His crosier has a white crook and a green staff. He also held a book, which is now lost. Beneath, *Scs*(·)*Athanasius*(·).

St. Athanasius, *c.* 297–373, became patriarch of Alexandria in 328. His life-work was the vindication of the true Faith against Arianism. He is venerated as one of the four great Greek Doctors.

2. ST. BERNARD. The background of the canopy is red and of the pedestal is murrey. The blue background of the figure is powdered with the letter *B*. He wears a russet habit and green shoes. The two green objects above his hands appear to be later insertions. Named, *Scs · Bernard'* ·.

This figure represents St. Bernard of Clairvaux, 1091–1153.

3. A BISHOP. The background of the canopy is red and of the pedestal is murrey. The blue background of the figure is powdered with the letter *H*. He wears a white alb and a white chasuble with yellow-stain orphrey. His amice and dalmatic are green, and his shoes red. His crosier has a white crook and murrey staff. The red glass by his right hand appears to be an insertion. Beneath, *Scs* and scraps.

There is no means of telling who this bishop may be. If the background originally belonged to the figure, and if the figure is of an English bishop, he might be St. Hugh of Lincoln, 1140–1200, for Wykeham was appointed Archdeacon of Lincoln in 1363. If the figure represents a foreign bishop, he may be St. Hilary of Poitiers, *ob.* 368, St. Hilary of Arles, *c.* 400–49, or St. Hypatius of Gangra, *ob. c.* 325. St. Hilary of Poitiers and St. Hypatius were both champions of the Faith against Arianism.

4. A BISHOP. The background of the canopy is red and of the pedestal is murrey. The blue background of the figure is powdered with the letter *B*. The bishop wears a white alb and a white chasuble with yellow-stain orphrey. His amice, dalmatic, and shoes are murrey. His crosier has a white crook and green shaft. Beneath, *Scs Bris, ii*. The last two letters probably come from the word *collegii*. The saint's name was at one time in the west window of this aisle, lower tier, light 2.

St. Brice, *ob.* 444, succeeded St. Martin as Bishop of Tours. He is depicted in fifteenth-century glass at Wiggenhall St. Mary Magdalene, Norfolk.

Across the pedestals in the lower part of the window are pieces of inscriptions, *S, rate p Willmo Wynton fud, col, Wynton fudator', istius coll.*

SOUTH AISLE. WEST WINDOW

TRACERIES. The angels are feathered and covered with eyes. Each angel has four wings. They wear diadems on their heads and knotted scarves round their necks. One hand is raised, with the other hand the angel grasps his wings. In the two upper lights, the left-hand angel is set against a blue background, the right-hand angel against a red background. They stand on murrey pedestals. Beneath, *Seraphyn*. The four lower figures are set against alternating murrey and purple backgrounds and stand upon green pedestals.

MAIN LIGHTS. UPPER TIER

1. St. MARY OF EGYPT. The backgrounds of the canopy and figure are blue, the background of the figure being powdered with the letter *E*. The background of the pedestal is purple. St. Mary wears a green robe and a white mantle with hood drawn over her head. She has a murrey nimbus and red shoes. She holds a murrey book. Beneath, *Maria · Egipcii ·*.

St. Mary of Egypt was not infrequently represented in English medieval art. Figures of her and of St. Mary Magdalene in a window of Bredon church, Worcestershire, are notable examples of early fourteenth-century glass-painting.

2. BARUCH. The backgrounds of the canopy and figure are blue, the background of the figure being powdered with the letter *M*. The background of the pedestal is red. Baruch wears a green robe, murrey mantle, yellow-brown headgear, and pink shoes. His scroll bears *Post · hec · in · tris · uisus · est · & · cū · hom · cōusatus · est* (Baruch iii. 38, *Post haec in terris visus est, et cum hominibus conversatus est*, 'After this he did shew himself upon earth, and conversed with men'). Beneath, *(B)aruc · ppheta ·*.

In fifteenth-century glass at Oxborough, Norfolk, Baruch has a text from Baruch iii. 35.

3. JONAH. The backgrounds of the canopy and figure are red, the background of the figure being powdered with the letter *I*. The background of the pedestal is purple. Jonah wears a white robe, green mantle, purple headgear and shoes, and blue hose. His scroll bears *Hebreus · ego · (sum · & · dominum) dm̄ · celi · ego · timeo* (Jonah i. 9, 'I am an Hebrew, and I fear the Lord, the God of heaven'). Beneath, *Ionas · ppheta ·*.

On the ceiling in Abingdon church Jonah's text is from Jonah ii. 3.

4. St. MARY MAGDALENE. The backgrounds of the canopy and base are blue. The red background of the figure is powdered

with the letter *M*. Mary Magdalene wears a blue robe, white mantle, and brown shoes. She has a purple nimbus. She holds forward a tress of her hair with her left hand: in her right hand is a purple object which should be the box or pot of ointment. Beneath, *Maria · Iacobi ·.*

This name was below Ezekiel when he stood in the place occupied by Jonah.

St. Mary Magdalene is not uncommonly shown in glass and on alabasters holding her hair forward in this way: it was a kind of secondary emblem. At least as early as the time of St. Gregory the Great the Church identified her with the woman that was a sinner. According to Matthew xxvi. 7 and Mark xiv. 3, Christ was anointed by an unnamed woman in the house of Simon at Bethany; according to John xiii. 3, by Mary the sister of Lazarus. According to Luke vii. 37, there was an earlier but similar anointing in Galilee.

The name *Maria Salome* was seen by Winston in light 2 of the upper tier of the east window of the north aisle. The representation of the 'Holy Kindred' grew out of a desire to enhance the cult of St. Anne and belief in the perpetual virginity of the Blessed Virgin Mary. It seems to have made its appearance late in the eleventh century in either Normandy or England. It became popular, but was subject to strong condemnation. St. Anne was accorded three husbands: by each she had a daughter called Mary. By Joachim she bore the Blessed Virgin Mary: by Cleophas, Mary who married Alphaeus and had children, SS. James the Less, Simon, Jude, and Joseph Justus; by Salome, Mary who married Zebedee and had children, SS. James Major and John Evangelist. This belief made it necessary to suppose that Salome was a man rather than a woman.[1] The name *Maria Iacobi* would seem to be a substitute for the more usual *Maria Cleophae*; that is to say 'Mary (the mother) of James (the Less)' instead of 'Mary (the daughter) of Cleophas'.

It is possible that the figure named St. Mary of Egypt in light 1 is in fact the figure of *Maria Iacobi* or *Maria Salome* and that the figure on a background powdered with the letter *M* and holding a palm in light 5 of the lower tier of the east window of this aisle represents St. Mary of Egypt.[2] If this is so, the figures were placed on the wrong backgrounds during some early restoration.

---

[1] M. R. James, 'The Salomites', *Journ. Theological Studies*, xxxv. 287–97.

[2] St. Mary of Egypt holds a palm in the Bredon glass; but as an emblem the palm generally indicates no more (except in the case of St. John Evangelist) than a saintly life (Revelation vii. 9).

LOWER TIER

1. ST. MARTHA. The backgrounds of the canopy and figure are red, the background of the figure being powdered with the letter *M*. The background of the pedestal is blue. Martha wears a blue robe and a white mantle and veil, and has a purple nimbus. Beneath, *Sēa · Martha ·*.

2. PARTS OF FIGURES OF A FEMALE SAINT AND A BISHOP. The background of the canopy is blue. The red background of the figures is powdered with the letter *C* and two specimens of the letter *B*. The background of the pedestal is murrey. The upper part of the light contains part of a figure of a female saint. She wears a blue robe and a white mantle and veil. The mantle is powdered with the letter *C* crowned and stained yellow. She has a purple nimbus and holds a purple book. In the lower part of the light there is part of the figure of a bishop. He wears a white alb and chasuble. His dalmatic is green and his shoes are blue. The shaft of his crosier is purple. Beneath, *Sēs · Anselmus ·*.

This name was at one time associated with the figure now in the west window of the north aisle, upper tier, light 3, but once in the south window of the south aisle, lower tier, light 4.

3. A QUEEN. The background of the canopy is red. The blue background of the figure is powdered with the letter *E*. The background of the pedestal is murrey. The queen wears a red robe with white sleeves. Her white mantle, which is diapered with the letter *E*, has a green ornamental band on the shoulders. The cord which held the mantle in place is lost. Two ornamental fillets hang on either side of her face and she has a red nimbus. In her left hand she holds a red book and in her right hand a sceptre with a golden floriated top and yellow-stain shaft. Beneath, the name is made up thus, *Sēa E, th, laca, a.*

Earlier writers have not hesitated to identify this figure with St. Etheldreda, who, according to Purnell's plan, was depicted on the south side of the choir. Yet the identification is untenable. St. Etheldreda is invariably shown in the habit of a nun, with a crown over her veil, and holding a crosier as the first abbess of Ely. The figure in light 4 makes it yet more sure that she was depicted in this way. The same considerations rule out such saints as Etheldreda's sister Ethelburga and niece Ermenilda, Edburga of Winchester, and Elfleda of Glastonbury. If the figure represents one of the early English saints, it may depict St. Etheldwitha, wife of King Alfred. After his death she retired to a nunnery which she had founded at Winchester.

4. St. Withburga and a bishop. The background of the canopy is blue. The backgrounds of the figures and pedestal are red, the background of the figures being powdered with the letter *W*. In the upper portion of the light is part of a figure of a female saint. She wears a blue robe and a white mantle, which is diapered with the letter *W* crowned. Her mantle has a golden ornamental band on the shoulders and is held in place by two red cords. She has on her head a white veil and a heavy golden crown. In her right hand she holds a purple book and in her left hand a golden sceptre. The lower part of her figure is lost and has been replaced by the lower part of a figure of a bishop. He wears a white alb and cope, a murrey stole and green shoes. The staff of his crosier is purple. Beneath, *Scs · Cuthbe(r)t' ·.*

St. Withburga was the youngest of the four saintly daughters of Anna, King of the East Angles: the others were St. Ethelburga, St. Etheldreda, and St. Sexburga. She founded a nunnery at East Dereham, Norfolk, where she peacefully lived. She is generally depicted with one or two does leaping up at her, as in fifteenth-century glass at Field Dalling and Salle, Norfolk.

Across the pedestals in the lower part of the window (Inserted capital letter *D*) *ate · p · Willmo · de · W*(scraps) *· epo · Wynton · fudator' · istius · collegii.*

There can be no better example of the fertility of invention displayed by the fourteenth-century glass-painters than the canopies and pedestals in the windows of this chapel. Winston counted eleven different types of canopy in the main lights.[1] The original plan was to have four designs in the main lights of each window, two in each tier, and to place them in alternate lights. This alternation of designs is now best seen in the lower part of the west window of the north aisle and in the upper parts of the east window of each aisle. It is unfortunate that the series in the lower part of the east window of each aisle is so incomplete. The alternating designs may have run right through both windows. The pedestals beneath the four crucifixes differ from the rest: they each contain a niche in which an old man (perhaps Adam) is seated.

Although generalizations about the colour-scheme of the windows can be only tentative because of the incompleteness of the various series, it is probable that in most, if not all, of the windows one colour was put behind the canopy and pedestal, and another behind the figure, and these two colours alternated

[1] 'The Painted Glass in New College Chapel and Hall, Oxford', 158.

in the adjoining light. In the Apostles series the colours of the robes, with the exception of those worn by SS. James the Greater and Philip, alternate with the colours of the backgrounds of the figures. The mantles are, with the same two exceptions, white. White is almost always used for the robes of the patriarchs and prophets, although here, too, there are exceptions, as in the figures of Baruch, Isaiah, Jeremiah, and Seth. These exceptions may be due to later mending or rearrangement, or it may be that in one window a different colour-scheme was used. The windows of the choir must have been strongly contrasted in their colour-schemes, and there certainly cannot have been any suggestion of monotony. The general effect of the windows devoted to the popes, archbishops, and bishops must have been like shimmering silver. The general effect of the windows containing the female saints would have been of great richness, with red, blue, and white as the predominant colours, and other colours, such as green, murrey, purple, and yellow, used to heighten the effect.

The decoration of the backgrounds of the figures with initial letters of this kind is without parallel. It was not unusual for a glass-painter to ornament the backgrounds with leaded-in patterns, but here the shape and size of the pieces and the design of a crowned initial letter are exactly like the borderwork constantly used elsewhere during this period. The glass-painter made one exception: behind the figure of St. Catherine he put crowned catherine-wheels instead of crowned initials K. It will also be noticed that he has usually painted a black pattern on the blue glass, but has only occasionally patterned the red glass. The patterns on the garments, especially on the mantles of the saints in the east window of each aisle, are ambitious and successful. The initial letters on the robe of St. John (as well as on the robes of some female saints) have already been noticed. Other notable patterns are the fighting cocks on the mantle of St. Bartholomew, the flying dragons on the mantles of SS. Philip and Simon, and the pairs of lions on the mantle of the Blessed Virgin Mary in light 4 of the east window of the south aisle.

It is remarkable that the faces of some of the figures, such as SS. Athanasius, Germanus, and Mary of Egypt have been cut into many diagonal strips. The probable reason for this is that during the 1895–1900 restoration Messrs. James Powell and Sons decided that the faces should be plated. The uneven surface of the glass made plating impossible unless the glass was cut into pieces.

THE GREAT WEST WINDOW

The upper main lights and the tracery lights contain a representation of the Nativity. The Virtues in the lower main lights are as follows: 1. Temperance. 2. Fortitude. 3. Faith. 4. Charity. 5. Hope. 6. Justice. 7. Prudence.

THE CHOIR WINDOWS. SOUTH SIDE

Reading from the east:

I. Traceries. *Cherubyn.* Main lights. Upper tier. 1. Bishop. 2. Bishop. The crook of his crosier is old. 3. Bishop. The crook of his crosier is old. 4. Archbishop. The top of his archiepiscopal cross is old. Lower tier. 1. Male saint. 2. Bishop. The crook of his crosier is old. 3. Pope. 4. Bishop. The crook of his crosier is old.

II. Traceries. *Dnaciois* (Dominations). Main lights. Upper tier. 1. Archbishop. The top of his archiepiscopal cross is old. 2. Bishop. 3. Male saint with book. 4. St. Laurence. Lower tier. 1. Archbishop. The top of his archiepiscopal cross is old. 2. Bishop. The crook of his crosier is old. 3. Bishop. Part of the crook of his crosier is old. 4. Cardinal.

III. Traceries. *Seraphyn.* Main lights. Upper tier. 1. Male saint, but without nimbus. 2. Archbishop. The top of his archiepiscopal cross is old: it has a figure of the crucified Christ upon it. 3. Bishop. 4. Bishop. Lower tier. 1. Female saint. 2. A royal personage with a sceptre and church. 3. Female saint with a book. 4. St. Catherine with a wheel and palm.

IV. Traceries. *Troni.* Main lights. Upper tier. 1. Pope. 2. St. John Evangelist with a chalice. 3. St. Paul with a sword. 4. Bishop. Lower tier. 1. Female saint. 2. Female saint with book and palm. 3. St. Agnes with a lamb. 4. St. Cecilia with a lute.

V. Traceries. *Principal.* Main lights. Upper tier. 1. Bishop. 2. Richly-dressed personage with sceptre. 3. Richly-dressed personage with sceptre. 4. Pope. Lower tier. 1. Female saint. 2. St. Helena with cross. 3. Female saint with sceptre and book. 4. Female saint with sword. At the bottom of this light: *W. Price has Fenestras reparavit. A° Dⁿⁱ 1740.*

Many of the smaller tracery openings in these windows contain their original glass *in situ*. The glass is painted with angels, grotesques, and floral devices. The canopies are of two designs only. One scheme of alternation is used in the two easternmost windows, another in the other windows. The most complete canopies remain in the lower lights of the third and fourth window from the east.

THE CHOIR WINDOWS. NORTH SIDE

Reading from the east:

I. Traceries. Six figures, much restored, of the Wise Virgins holding lighted lamps and set against alternating red and blue backgrounds.[1] Beneath the two upper figures, *Vir · gi · nes*. Main lights. Upper tier. 1. St. Philip with cross. 2. St. James the Greater with pilgrim's staff. 3. St. Andrew with cross. 4. St. Bartholomew with knife. Lower tier. 1. St. Paul with sword. 2. St. Barnabas with scroll. 3. St. Jude with halbert. 4. St. Matthias with halbert.

On the bases of the shafts of the canopy in lower tier, 4:

$(1)765$ *W*: *Pec(kitt)*
                           pin(xit)

II. Traceries. *Angeli*. Main lights. 1. St. James Minor with a club. 2. St. Thomas with a spear. 3. St. Simon with a saw. 4. St. Matthew with a T-square and scroll. Lower tier. 1. St. John Evangelist with a chalice. 2. Jesus Christ. 3. The Blessed Virgin Mary. 4. St. Peter with two keys.

The figures are named upon scrolls at the bottom of the lights. Below the figure of the Blessed Virgin Mary is a shield bearing *Argent, on a chevron sable three quatrefoils or*. On a scroll around the shield, *Iohannes Eyre A.M. hujus hosp. Soc.*[2]

III. Traceries. *Archangeli*. Main lights. Upper tier. 1. Micah. 2. Nahum. 3. Habakkuk. 4. Zephaniah. Lower tier. 1. Jacob. 2. Judah. 3. Moses. 4. Aaron.

IV. Traceries. *uir-tu-tes*. Main lights. Upper tier. 1. Joel. 2. Amos. 3. Obadiah. 4. Jonah. Lower tier. 1. Methuselah. 2. Noah. 3. Abraham. 4. Isaac.

V. Traceries. *Potestates*. Main lights. Upper tier. 1. Baruch. 2. Hosea. 3. Daniel. 4. Ezekiel. Lower tier. 1. Adam. 2. Eve. 3. Seth. 4. Enoch.

At the bottom of the left-hand shaft of the canopy which stands over Adam is the date *1774*.

Some fourteenth-century glass is incorporated in the figures and their settings in the tracery lights.

The figures in the main lights of windows III–V are not named. There are some variations of detail and design from the figures in Rebecca's sketch, especially in window IV. Rebecca himself probably made these alterations when he drew the cartoons.

The following inscription, running across the pedestals in the

[1] See above, p. 71.   [2] See above, p. 21.

lower part of the window, is to be seen in all the windows except the two easternmost on the north side: *Orate · p̄ · Willm̄o · de · Wykhm̄ · epō · Wȳton · fūdatore · istius · Collegii.*

2. OTHER PARTS OF THE COLLEGE

THE WINDOW OVER THE STAIRWAY TO THE HALL

The heraldic glass in this window was removed from the hall windows in 1865.

NORTHERN TRACERY LIGHT. *Party per fess or and gules, a double-headed eagle displayed sable having on its breast a demi-rose and a demi-sun conjoined in one and counter-changed of the field,* for Knight. Date, sixteenth century.

William Knight, 1476–1547, became a Fellow of New College in 1493. He was Bishop of Bath and Wells, 1541–7. These arms were assigned to him in 1514.[1] At that time he was Protonotary of the Apostolic See and Ambassador from Henry VIII to the Emperor. The arms are also to be seen in glass of about the same date in the north aisle of the choir of Wells cathedral.

SOUTHERN TRACERY LIGHT. *Quarterly, 1. Argent, a pelican in her piety vert and a bordure indented argent and vert,* for Sherburne, *2 and 3, Argent, a lion rampant vert,* for Sherburne of Stonyhurst. *4. Argent, an eagle displayed vert.* Date, early sixteenth century.

The tinctures of the arms in the first quarter are usually reversed.

Robert Sherburne became a Fellow of New College in 1474 and Bishop of Chichester, 1508–36.

SOUTHERN MAIN LIGHT

1. *Argent, two chevrons sable between three roses gules,* for Wykeham. Date, late fourteenth century.

2. France and England quarterly. The shield is flanked by the letters *E.P.,* for Edward VI when Prince of Wales. It is surrounded by a wreath and surmounted by a crown. Date, early sixteenth century.

The arms are now incomplete. Both the 'England' quarters have gone: one of them was *differenced with a label of three points argent.* One fleur-de-lis is missing from the arms of France in the fourth quarter.

3. *Azure, a sword and a key saltirewise argent, in chief a mitre argent,* for the See of Winchester.

[1] A transcription of the grant of arms is preserved in the College of Heralds and is listed Vincent MS. 88. 1.

Le Couteur notes that these arms, which he calls 'the ancient arms of the see of Winchester', occur several times in glass of the middle of the fifteenth century in tracery lights of the northern clerestory of the choir of Winchester cathedral.[1]

MIDDLE MAIN LIGHT

1. *Azure, an archiepiscopal staff or surmounted by a pallium argent charged with four crosses patée fitched sable,* for the See of Canterbury, impaling *Gules, a fess or between a goat's head erased in chief and three scallops in base argent,* for Warham. Date, sixteenth century.

The arms, which are within a wreath and surmounted by a mitre, are now incomplete. The pallium, staff, goat's head, and scallops have gone and have been replaced by white and yellow glass. The yellow fess is of modern glass.

William Warham, Fellow of New College, 1475, Archbishop of Canterbury, 1504–32, gave to the College lands in Kingsclere and Swalcliffe.

2. France and England quarterly, surrounded by the Garter. Supporters, a red dragon and a white greyhound. For Henry VIII. Date, sixteenth century.

3. *Azure, on a cross or between four griffins' heads erased argent a rose gules,* for Gardiner. Date, second half of the sixteenth century.

The arms are surrounded by the Garter and surmounted by a modern mitre.

Stephen Gardiner, 1483?–1555, was consecrated Bishop of Winchester on 27 November 1532.

NORTHERN LIGHT

1. *Argent, a cross gules,* for St. George. Date, late fourteenth century.

2. *Gules, three crowns in pale or,* probably for Ireland. Date, late fourteenth century.

3. France and England quarterly. Date, late fourteenth century.

THE WARDEN'S LODGINGS

THE GALLERY

1. The arms of Wykeham surrounded by the Garter and surmounted by a mitre. Date, sixteenth century. The mitre and much of the white glass in the shield are of later date.

2. *Gules, two keys argent and or addorsed and erect, with a sword argent hilted and pommelled or set saltirewise between them,* for the

---

[1] *Ancient Glass in Winchester,* 32.

See of Winchester, *impaling* Gardiner. The shield is surrounded by the Garter, which is now incomplete. Date, sixteenth century.

Here also are two square quarries. One is painted with the arms of Wykeham and the other with this inscription, *MANER MAKYTH MAN QD. BYSHOP WYKHAM.*[1] The arms and the inscription are set within ornamental borders. Date, late sixteenth century.

STAIRCASE WINDOW

1. *Gules, five lozenges conjoined in fess argent each charged with a scallop sable*, for Cheney. Date, nineteenth century.

Thomas Cheney, who became a Fellow of New College in 1673 and who died in 1724, gave £30 towards the new buildings at New College.

2. *Argent, on a bend sable three roses of the field, in chief a crescent or*, for Carey. Date, nineteenth century.

John Carey, who became a Fellow of New College in 1714 and who died in 1764, left property in Westminster 'in incrementum portionis D. Custodis' and £100 to the College.

LIGHTS OVER THE FRONT DOOR

Here are two quarries with these arms painted in enamels: *Quarterly, 1.* Wykeham, *2 and 3. Argent, ten torteaux, 4. Argent, a cross couped between four crosses patée fitched sable.* The shield is surrounded by mantling and surmounted by a helmet and a crest, *A bird proper with a snake azure.* On a scroll: *PRUDENTIA · INNOCENS.* Date, probably eighteenth century.

These arms occur again on two shields in the west window of the Old Library of Trinity College, Oxford. The quarterings cannot be identified and may be fanciful. The shields were given to Trinity College by Jane Warton soon after her brother Thomas's death in 1790. Thomas may have given the quarries to New College.

[1] The motto is first recorded by Thomas Chaundler, Warden 1453–75, who gives it as *Mores componunt hominem* (New College MS. 288). On the small seal of the College, *temp.* John London, Warden, 1526–42, it appears as *MANNER MAKYTH MAN.* In the third window from the east on the north side of the nave of Bradford Peverell church, Dorset, there is sixteenth-century glass surrounding the arms of Wykeham. The shield of arms is encircled with the Garter and surmounted by a mitre. On a scroll behind the mitre is *Manare: makythe: man.* On scrolls below are the words · *q': Willam: Wykkam, Wykkam:, Willam.* The glass was considerably restored by N. J. Cottingham. The shield of arms is entirely new. The mitre is modern, but its labels are old. Part of the original background of diapered murrey glass remains; the rest is of modern red glass. The words *Churche Patron* were once to be seen below the shield (J. Hutchins, *The History and Antiquities of the County of Dorset*, London, 1863, ii. 537). This glass came from the old church and was not brought from New College.

THE OLD BURSARY

The eastern window contains an incomplete roundel of late fifteenth-century date. It shows a peewit holding a scroll in its beak. The scroll is inscribed, *Redde · quod · debes ·*. The peewit has been seen as a pun on 'pay it'.

THE MUNIMENT ROOM

Amongst the glass preserved here is the following:

1. Two panels, each showing a Wise Virgin, from the tracery lights of the easternmost window on the northern side of the chapel.

2. Two heads of the Deity, one of fourteenth-century date, the other of fifteenth-century date.

3. The feet of Christ pierced by a single nail and showing drops of blood. They were found in a tracery light of one of the chapel windows in 1934 and presumably belong to one of the crucifixes in the eastern windows of the aisles.

4. Two crowned letters *W*, three crowned letters *A*, and two crowned catherine-wheels from backgrounds: two initial letters *S* from names or inscriptions: pieces of inscriptions, *iel, leg, tōn, tor', Wil, will, ·uir'*.

5. Late fourteenth-century patterned quarries and pieces of white borderwork. These were found under the floor of the Library in June 1950 and are probably remains of the original glazing of its windows.

6. Part of a fifteenth-century quarry showing a portcullis. It was found under the floor of the Library in June 1950.

7. Parts of two small fifteenth-century crucifixes. These may have been parts of archiepiscopal crosses.[1]

8. Part of a fifteenth-century shield painted with the Instruments of the Passion.

9. A piece of glass showing a group of male heads: late fifteenth-century.

10. A piece of diapered drapery from a small seated figure of fifteenth-century date.

11. Two quarries with shields of arms similar to those above the front door of the Warden's Lodgings, but without the mantling, helmet, crest, and motto.

12. Part of a seventeenth-century shield with the arms of Wykeham, surrounded by the Garter, and flanked by the letters (*W*)*W*.

13. *ANNA REGINA*, done in yellow letters on white glass.

14. A piece of painted glass on the outside surface of which is

---

[1] See above, p. 91.

scratched *Richard Fleming Glazer 1775 Willm Curtice Glazier 1777 (Li)ght Leaded 1777.*[1]

THE HALL

The main lights of the hall windows contain heraldic glass. The shields are set upon patterned glass cut into quarries or decorative shapes and are accompanied by descriptive labels. Each main tracery light holds a half-length figure, which is named. Round the bottom of all the upper main lights and round the bottom of all the lower main lights there are inscriptions which read respectively.

✠ *Agimus tibi gratias omnipotens Deus pro fundatore nostro Gulielmo de Wykeham reliquisque quorum beneficiis hic ad pietatem et ad studia literarum alimur rogantes ut nos his donis tuis ad nominis tui honorem recte utentes ad resurrectionis tuae gloriam perducamur immortalem per Jesum Christum Dominum nostrum Amen.*

Oculi omnium spectant in te Domine Tu das iis escam in tempore opportuno Tu aperis manum (et) imples omne animal benedictione tua Benedictus sit Deus in donis suis Et sanctus in omnibus operibus ejus Adjutorium nostrum est in nomine Domini Qui fecit coelum et terram sit nomen Domini benedictum Ex hoc nunc usque in saeculum benedicite (Domino) Amen Mensae coelestis participes nos facias Rex aeternae gloriae.

These sentences are based upon graces once said before and after dinner and supper at New College.[2]

The main lights of the westernmost window on each side of the hall have shields bearing royal arms with names and dates beneath. All the shields except one are surmounted by badges showing lions standing upon crowns. The lion on each alternate shield is shown as 'guardant'. The other windows contain the arms and names of benefactors of the College. The arms in the upper row both above and below the transom are of episcopal benefactors and are surmounted by mitres.

A window in the roof also contains stained glass.

NORTH SIDE

I. Tracery light. King Edward III.

Main lights

1. France (ancient) and England quarterly. *Edward III: Rex · 1327.*

2. *Azure, a cross patonce between four martlets or,* for Edward the

---

[1] See above, p. 39.
[2] The graces are printed in *Reliquiae Hearnianae (Extracts from the Diaries of Thomas Hearne),* ed. P. Bliss, Oxford, 1857, ii. 910–12.

H

Confessor, *per pale* France and England quarterly. *Ricardus II: Rex · 1377.*

3. *Quarterly, 1 and 4.* England, *2 and 3, Quarterly, 1 and 2. Or, a lion rampant sable,* for Hainault, *2 and 3. Or, a lion rampant gules,* for Holland. *Philippa Edwardi Conjux.*

4. *Per pale of three, 1.* Edward the Confessor. *2.* France and England quarterly. *3. Quarterly, 1 and 4. Argent, an eagle displayed with two heads sable,* for Germany, *2 and 3. Gules, a lion rampant queue-fourché argent crowned or,* for Bohemia. *Anna Ricardi Conjux.*

5. France (ancient) and England quarterly, *with a label of five points argent. Edward · Princeps Walliae 1343.*

The lion on the badge is *differenced with a label of five points argent* and stands upon *a cap of pretence gules trimmed ermine.*

6. France (ancient) and England quarterly. *Henricus: IV · Rex: 1399.*

7. France and England quarterly. *Henricus: VI · Rex: 1422.*

8. France and England quarterly. *Edwardus: IV · Rex: 1461.*

II. TRACERY LIGHT. William of Wykeham.

Main lights.

1. *Azure, an episcopal staff in pale or, ensigned with a cross patée argent surmounted by a pall argent edged and fringed or, charged with four crosses patée fitched sable,* for the See of Canterbury, *impaling Or, a chevron between three cinquefoils gules,* for Chicheley. *Hen: Chicheley Socius 1389.*

2. See of Canterbury impaling Warham. *Gul: Warham Socius 1475.*

3. *Gules, a chevron between three scallops argent,* for Hardinge. *Clem. Hardinge Socius 1482.*

4. *Ermine, on a cross engrailed purple five martlets or,* for Millinge. *Thos. Millinge Socius 1490.*

5. *Gules, two keys the wards in chief addorsed in bend the uppermost or the other argent a sword the point in chief interposed between them in bend sinister argent hilted and pommelled or,* for the See of Winchester, *impaling* Wykeham. *Gul. de Wykeham Fundator 1386.*

6. *Gules, two lions passant guardant or, on a chief azure the Virgin and Child or,* for the See of Lincoln, *impaling Gules, a cross botonny or,* for Bokyngham. *Joh. Bokyngham Ep. Lincoln 1363.*

7. *Argent, eleven mullets azure,* for Phipps. *Joh. Phipps Socius 1476.*

8. *Sable, three swords in fess argent hilted and pommelled or in chief a crescent or,* for Rawlins. *Christ. Rawlins Socius 1537.*

III. TRACERY LIGHT. Richard II.

Main lights.

1. See of Winchester *impaling Lozengy sable and ermine on a chief ermine three lilies proper*, for Waynflete. *Gul: de Waynflete Inform. Winton 1430.*

2. *Gules, three leopards' heads reversed jessant-de-lis or two and one*, for the See of Hereford, *impaling Argent, on a fess sable between three roses gules a lily proper*, for Mayhew. *Ric: Mayhew Socius 1459.*

3. *Argent, on a bend sable cottised gules three lozenges ermine*, for Ryves. *Geo: Ryves Socius 1580.*

4. *Azure, three pheasants or*, for Reade. *Ric. Reade Socius 1530.*

5. See of Lincoln *impaling Azure, two chevronels or between three roses argent*, for Russell. *Joh. Russell Socius 1449.*

6. *Azure, a saltire per saltire quarterly counterchanged argent and or*, for the See of Bath and Wells, *impaling Argent, on a fess sable between in chief three stags' heads gules attired or and in base three pheons sable a mitre or*, for Beckington. *Tho: Bekinton Socius 1408.*

7. *Argent, two bars gules*, for Preston. *Nic. Preston Socius 1721.*

8. *Gules, a fess chequy or and azure between ten billets argent*, for Lee. *Lanc. Car. Lee Socius 1785.*

IV. TRACERY LIGHT. Archbishop Chicheley.

Main lights.

1. See of Winchester *impaling Party per chevron or and gules between three roses counterchanged, on a chief gules three hour-glasses or*, for White. *Joh. White Socius 1527.*

2. *Sable, three crowns in pale or*, for the See of Bristol, *impaling Argent, two bars engrailed azure between three roses gules slipped vert*, for Holyman. *Joh: Holyman Socius 1512.*

3. *Gules, three martlets or, a chief vair*, for Bailey. *Hen. Bailey Socius 1536.*

4. *Argent, a lion passant sable, on a chief sable three mullets of six points argent*, for Ball. *Rob. Ball Socius 1571.*

5. See of Bath and Wells *impaling Sable, a bend between six crosses crosslet fitched or*, for Lake. *Arth. Lake Custos 1613.*

6. *Azure, three mitres with their labels, two and one, or*, for the See of Norwich, *impaling Vert, a lion rampant or langued gules debruised of a fess or*, for Jane. *Tho. Jane Socius 1456.*

7. *Argent, on a chevron between three billets azure a fret or impaling Azure, two bars between six leopards' faces argent*, for Dell. *Joh: Dell Socius 1775.*

8. *Azure, a stag lodged argent,* for Downes. *Ric: Downes Socius 1796.*

SOUTH SIDE

I. TRACERY LIGHT. Queen Victoria.

Main lights.

1. France (ancient) and England quarterly. *Henricus: VII · Rex: 1485.*
2. France (ancient) and England quarterly. *Ricardus: III · Rex: 1483.*
3. France (ancient) and England quarterly. *Henricus: VIII · Rex: 1509.*
4. *Quarterly, I and IV grand quarters, Quarterly, 1 and 4. Gules, a castle triple-towered or,* for Castile, *2 and 3. Argent, a lion rampant gules,* for Leon: *II and III grand quarters, Or, four pallets gules,* for Aragon, *impaling* a version of the arms of Sicily, *impaling* France and England quarterly. *Maria. Regina: 1553.*
5. France (ancient) and England quarterly. *Elizabetha · Regina: 1558.*
6. *Quarterly, 1 and 4.* France and England quarterly, *2.* Scotland. *3.* Ireland. *Carolus: II · Rex: 1649.*
7. The Royal Arms, as borne 1814–37. *Georgius: III · Rex: 1760.*
8. *Quarterly, 1 and 4.* England. *2.* Scotland. *3.* Ireland. *Victoria · Regina: 1837.*

II. TRACERY LIGHT. Bishop Waynflete.

Main lights.

1. See of Winchester *impaling* France and England quarterly, *within a bordure compony argent and azure,* for Beaufort. The shield is surmounted by a cardinal's hat. *Hen. Beaufort · Cardinalis: 1405.*
2. See of Canterbury *impaling Quarterly sable and or, a cross saltire engrailed and counterchanged,* for Pole. The shield is surmounted by a cardinal's hat. *Reg. Pole Cardinalis 1405.*
3. *Argent, four lozenges in pale gules, a bordure azure charged with eight crosses patée fitched or,* for Pinke. *Robt. Pinke Custos 1617.*
4. *Barry of six or and sable, a canton gules,* for Woodward. *Mich. Woodward Custos 1658.*
5. *Azure, an episcopal staff in pale argent ensigned with a cross patée or surmounted by a pall or edged and fringed argent, charged with four crosses patée fitched sable,* for the See of Dublin, *impaling Azure, a*

lion's face between three crowns or, for Cranley. *Thos. Cranley Custos 1389.*

6. The See of Dublin *impaling Or, a chevron vert,* for Inge. *Hugo Inge Socius 1484.*

7. *Gules, three pears or, on a chief or a lion issuant sable,* for Parrott. *Car · Parrott Socius 1732.*

8. *Argent, on a bend sable three roses of the field, in chief a crescent gules,* for Carey. *Joh: Carey Socius 1714.*

III. TRACERY LIGHT. Henry VI.

Main lights.

1. See of Canterbury *impaling Azure, an eagle displayed argent differenced with a cross azure,* for Howley. *Gul. Howley Socius 1785.*

2. See of Winchester *impaling Ermine, two chevrons gules,* for Sumner. *C.R. Sumner Ep. Wint. 1827.*

3. *Gules, three scallops and a bordure engrailed argent,* for Erle. *Gul. Erle Socius 1813.*

4. *Sable, a chevron between three pheons argent embrued gules,* for Williams. *Dau. Williams Custos 1840.*

5. *Gules, two swords in saltire argent hilted and pommelled or, the dexter surmounted by the sinister,* for the See of London, *impaling Sable, a wolf salient argent langued gules,* for Lowth. *Rob: Lowth Socius 1713.*

6. See of Bath and Wells *impaling Ermine, three crescents gules,* for Ken. *Tho: Ken Socius 1659.*

7. *Azure, three etoiles in bend double cottised argent,* for Bridle. *Ioh: Bridle Socius 1726.*

8. *Gules, a pelican in her piety or, on a chief argent a hunting-horn between two cinquefoils sable, in base a fleur-de-lis or,* for Duncan. *P.B. Duncan Socius 1792.*

THE WINDOW IN THE ROOF

The eastern and western lights contain roundels. Some are painted with the letters *v.r.*: they are flanked by the mottoes, *Dieu et mon Droit,* and surmounted by lions standing on crowns. Others are painted with the initial letter *W* and are surmounted by mitres.

IV

THE 'TREE OF JESSE' IN YORK MINSTER

THE west window of New College chapel and the east window of Winchester College chapel both have seven main lights, divided by a transom. They were filled with representations of the 'Tree of Jesse', which were very alike. The Winchester College 'Tree of Jesse' was replaced by a faithful copy which shows the original designs of the windows.[1] The panels in the tops of the three middle lights show a Crucifix with figures of the Blessed Virgin Mary and St. John Evangelist. The two panels immediately below the Crucifix contain the Blessed Virgin and Child. The lowest range of panels show, from left to right, 1. The Annunciation, with a kneeling figure of William of Wykeham. 2. The Holy Trinity, with a kneeling figure of King Edward III. 3–5. The recumbent figure of Jesse. At his head kneel i. *Carpentarius* ·, ii. *Willm̄s · Wynforde · lathomus* ·, iii. *Dn̄s Simon · Membury* ·. At his feet kneels *Thom̄s · op̄ator · isti' · vitri*. Above his feet an angel holding an open book. 6. St. John Baptist, with a kneeling figure of King Richard II. 7. The Blessed Virgin Mary and Child, with a kneeling figure of William of Wykeham. The rest of the two outermost lights are filled with ten figures of prophets. The rest of the other lights contain eighteen figures of kings and two figures of prophets. The two tracery lights immediately above the middle main light hold figures of SS. Peter and Paul. The two lights above them have figures of the Blessed Virgin Mary and St. John Baptist.[2] The light in the head of the window contains a representation of Christ in majesty. The rest of the tracery lights contained a 'Doom'.

As has been seen, the New College 'Tree of Jesse' was given to Peckitt in part payment for his glass.[3] There is no means of

---

[1] The story of the removal of the glass is told in *Ancient Glass in Winchester*, 69–71. A considerable amount of it was acquired by Evelyn John Shirley, who was a Wykehamist. He placed it in the windows of the mortuary chapel of his family in the grounds of Ettington Park, Warwickshire, the chapel being a restored transept of an otherwise ruined church. The glass was in place by 1825 (E. P. Shirley, *Lower Eatington: its Manor House and Church*, London, 1869, 70). It has since been acquired by Winchester College for replacement in the chapel. The figure of Joash passed into the possession of the Victoria and Albert Museum. Five other figures are in private possession in America.

[2] There were thus five representations of the Blessed Virgin Mary in the window, which recalls the fact that the College was called 'Saint Mary College of Winchester' and that New College was called 'St. Mary College of Winchester in Oxford'.

[3] See above, pp. 20–1.

telling how complete it was when he removed it from the window. Part of it is now in York minster and can be seen in the three-light window over the entrance to the Zouche chapel in the south aisle of the choir.

The vine-stems are white. White, yellow, green, murrey, and purple glass is used for the leaves and grapes. The figures are named upon scrolls. The backgrounds were alternately red and blue, but most of the red glass is now white, perhaps because the red 'flash' had become so corroded that it was scraped off to make the glass less opaque. It is impossible to be sure that the scrolls bearing names are now attached to the right figures; for instance, in the case of a king with the name *Ezechias* (fourth panel in the second light) the scroll certainly comes from a lost panel showing the prophet Ezechiel. The Winchester window is no certain guide in this matter, for the two windows were not identical in design. The lights have startling borders of Peckitt's making. Reading from left to right and from top to bottom, the figures in the main lights are as follows.

I. 1. *2amuel*. He wears green headgear. Very little of the rest of the figure remains: it is made up with white drapery, ornamented with a yellow-stain pattern, and murrey glass. The figure of Samuel from Winchester is now in America. In the copy he occupies the fifth panel (from the top) in the second light (from the left) and his name is spelt *Samuel*.

2. *Sedechias* (Zedekiah). He holds a sceptre. His robes are rather fragmentary. He wore an ermine tippet and, perhaps, a white mantle ornamented with a yellow-stain pattern. In the Winchester copy he occupies the top of the second light and his name is spelt in the same way.

3. *Ioathan rex*. The figure is fairly complete. The king holds a sceptre. He points to his scroll with his left hand. He wears a white robe, with yellow-stain ornamentation, and a green mantle with ermine tippet. He has white shoes patterned in black. In the Winchester copy he occupies the third panel in the second light and he is named in the same way.

4. *Manasses*. The figure is fairly complete. The king holds a sceptre. He points to his scroll with his right hand. His green robe has a yellow hem and is girded with a yellow belt. His mantle is of a light purple glass with ermine tippet and lining. The Winchester figure survives in an incomplete state and is unnamed. In the copy it occupies the second panel in the sixth light and is named in the same way.

5. *Daniel*. The figure is very fragmentary. The right hand is

now shown as pointing to the scroll and the left hand as resting on the breast. The robes are made up with murrey and pale purple glass. In the Winchester copy he occupies the second panel in the seventh light and he is named in the same way.

II. 1. *Ochozia(s)* (Hezekiah). The figure is very fragmentary. The king holds a sceptre. His left hand rests on his breast. His robes are made up with murrey and brick-red glass. The Winchester figure survives and is named *Ochozi(as)*. In the copy it occupies the third panel in the fifth light.

2. *Ioas: rex*. The figure is not complete. The sceptre is lost. He grasps his beard with his right hand. He wears a white robe ornamented with a yellow-stain pattern and girded with a yellow belt. His mantle and shoes are blue. The Winchester figure was acquired by the Victoria and Albert Museum. The copy occupies the third panel in the sixth light and is named in the same way.

3. *Iosias*. The figure is fragmentary. The king holds a sceptre in his left hand and he points to his scroll with his right hand. He has a white mantle with yellow-stain ornamentation, and a robe is suggested with blue glass. The Winchester figure survives in America. The copy is named in the same way as the New College figure and occupies the second panel in the second light.

4. *Ezechias*. A fairly complete figure of a king holding a sceptre. He has a white mantle with yellow-stain ornamentation, and white shoes. A robe is suggested with ruby glass. In the Winchester copy *Ezechiel ppha* occupies the second panel in the first light.

5. *Achaz rex*. The king has a sceptre in his left hand. He wears a white robe with yellow-stain ornamentation and girded with a yellow belt, a green mantle with ermine lining, and murrey shoes. Winchester College possesses part of its original figure of this king. In the copy he occupies the second panel in the third light and is named in the same way.

III. 1. *Abia rex*. The figure is very fragmentary. The king has robes made up of green glass and of white glass with yellow-stain ornamentation. He has blue shoes. In the Winchester copy he occupies the fourth panel in the fifth light and is named in the same way.

2. *Ioram rex*. The figure is fairly complete. The king is now shown as having his hands crossed upon his breast. He wears a white mantle with yellow-stain ornamentation and has green shoes. The Winchester figure survives in America. In the copy he occupies the third panel in the third light and is named in the same way.

3. *Jeconias:*. The figure is fairly complete. The king wears a white robe with yellow-stain ornamentation and girded with a yellow belt. The Winchester figure survives in America. In the copy he occupies the topmost panel in the sixth light and is named in the same way.

4. *Helias · pp(hā)*. The figure is incomplete. The prophet's left hand is raised to hold the end of the scroll which passes behind his head. He wears green headgear and shoes. His robes are made up of green glass and white drapery with yellow-stain ornamentation. In the Winchester copy he occupies the fifth panel in the first light and is named in the same way.

5. *Amos pphā*. The figure is incomplete. The prophet is now shown as having his hands crossed on his breast. His robe is made up of green glass and of white drapery with yellow-stain ornamentation. In the Winchester copy this prophet occupies the third panel in the seventh light and is named in the same way.

The topmost tracery light contains part of a figure of a king. He held a scroll which is made up of pieces of lettering. The piece which reads *us: p* belongs to the 'Tree of Jesse'. According to the Winchester copy, this must have come from the name *Heliseus pphā*; there the prophet occupied the fifth panel in the seventh light. The king wears a made-up green mantle with ermine tippet.

The large left-hand light contains vine-work and a made-up figure of St. John Baptist. This figure probably occupied a tracery light, as at Winchester.

The large right-hand light contains part of a figure of a king. He is named · *Amon · rex*. He holds a sceptre in his right hand and clasps his beard with his left hand. The figure is very much made up. In the Winchester copy Amon occupies the fifth panel from the top in the third light and is named *Amnon rex*.

The six tracery lights immediately above the main lights contain figures, including demons and ecclesiastics, from a 'Doom', and canopy work.

The prophets and kings which are portrayed in the Winchester copy, but which have not been named above are Absalom, Asa, David, Isaiah, Jeremiah, Jehoshaphat, Malachi, Micah, Nathan, Rehoboam, Solomon, Zechariah, and Zorobabel. The original figures of Absalom, Jehoshaphat, Micah, Nathan, and Zechariah went to Ettington Park and the original figure of Solomon went to America.

INDEX

PLATES

S. Pitcher

JUDAH   ADAM

ADAM

L. Banks

JUDAH

L. Banks

EVE

ENOCH

DANIEL   JEREMIAH

S. Pitcher

ST. ATHANASIUS   A BISHOP

L. Banks

PART OF A FIGURE OF ST. JOHN EVANGELIST
From the Series of the Twelve Apostles

L. Banks

A ROYAL SAINT

M. de Putron

WILLIAM OF WYKEHAM

A WISE VIRGIN

THE ORDER 'ANGELS'

INITIAL LETTERS FROM THE WINDOWS OF NEW COLLEGE CHAPEL

Drawn by Charles Winston

  H.M. Stationery Office

WINDOW OVER STAIRWAY TO THE HALL

S.

FIGURES ON THE SOUTH SIDE OF THE CHOIR
Painted by William Price

FIGURES ON THE SOUTH SIDE OF THE CHOIR
Painted by William Price

FIGURES ON THE NORTH SIDE OF THE CHOIR
Painted by William Peckitt

S. Pitcher

FIGURES ON THE NORTH SIDE OF THE CHOIR

Sts. Paul and Barnabas painted by William Raphael Eginton, Sts. Jude and Matthias painted by William Peckitt

ASHMOLEAN MUSEUM, OXFORD

Sketch by Sir Joshua Reynolds of 'Charity' for the West Window of New College Chapel

The West Window. The Nativity
From an engraving by G. S. and I. G. Facius

W. J. Green

YORK MINSTER, JECONIAS

ALL THE WINDOWS in the chapel of New College, Oxford, are filled with stained glass. The fourteenth-century glass in the ante-chapel is well known to students of English medieval art. William Price's windows on the south side of the choir and William Peckitt's windows on the north side occupy an important place in the history of English glass-painting. The 'Reynolds' window has been an object of admiration or curiosity ever since it was painted. Besides all the glass in the chapel, the College possesses good examples of heraldic glass dating from the fourteenth century to the nineteenth century.

This fine display is matched by an unusually complete body of records dating from the fourteenth century to recent times. Especially notable is the lively correspondence between the College and the various people concerned with the production of the eighteenth-century windows.

The book is divided into four parts. The first part is occupied by a history of the glass from the time of the building of the College to the replacement of the glass in the windows of the ante-chapel after the Second World War. The second part tells of three earlier descriptions of the glass. The third part is devoted to a detailed description of all the stained glass in the College. The fourth part contains an account of the 'Tree of Jesse' which is part of the original glazing of the great west window of the chapel and is now in a window of York Minster.

The illustrations have been carefully chosen to show the beauty of the medieval glass and the various styles of the eighteenth-century designers and glass-painters.